Working with HDV: Shoot, Edit, and Deliver Your High Definition Video

Chuck Gloman
Mark J. Pescatore, Ph.D.

ELSEVIER

AMSTERDAM • BOSTON • HEIDLEBERG • LONDON
NEW YORK • OXFORD • PARIS • SAN DIEGO
SAN FRANCISCO • SINGAPORE • SYDNEY • TOKYO
Focal Press is an imprint of Elsevier

Focal Press

Acquisitions Editor: Elinor Actipis
Project Manager: Brandy Lilly
Assistant Editor: Robin Weston
Marketing Manager: Christine Degon Veroulis
Cover Design: Eric Decicco
Technical Editor: Tim Kolb
Book Production: Borrego Publishing (www.borregopublishing.com)

Focal Press is an imprint of Elsevier
30 Corporate Drive, Suite 400, Burlington, MA 01803, USA
Linacre House, Jordan Hill, Oxford OX2 8DP, UK

 Recognizing the importance of preserving what has been written, Elsevier prints its books on acid-free
paper whenever possible.

Library of Congress Cataloging-in-Publication Data
Gloman, Chuck B.
  Working with HDV : shoot, edit, and deliver your high definition video / by Chuck Gloman and Mark J.
Pescatore.
     p. cm.
  Includes bibliographical references and index.
  ISBN-13: 978-0-240-80888-8 (pbk. : alk. paper)
  ISBN-10: 0-240-80888-6 (pbk. : alk. paper) 1. Video recording--Amateurs' manuals. 2. Digital video--
Editing--Amateurs' manuals. 3. Video recordings--Production and direction--Amateurs' manuals. 4. High
definition television--Amateurs' manuals. 5. High definition television--Standards--Amateurs' manuals. I.
Pescatore, Mark James. II. Title
  TR851.G545 2006
  778.59--dc22
                                    2006018658

British Library Cataloguing-in-Publication Data
A catalogue record for this book is available from the British Library.

ISBN 13: 978-0-240-80888-8
ISBN 10: 0-240-80888-6

For information on all Focal Press publications visit our website at www.books.elsevier.com

07 08 09 10   10 9 8 7 6 5 4 3 2 1

Printed in the United States of America

Working with HDV:
Shoot, Edit, and Deliver

Learner Services

Please return on or before the last date stamped below

CITY COLLEGE
NORWICH

1 0 SEP 2010

29 JUN 2012

Contents

Preface

The video industry changed forever in 2003. Four companies—Canon, Inc., Sharp Corporation, Sony Corporation, and Victor Company of Japan, Limited (JVC)—joined together to develop and introduce a new video format. However, this was not just another video format, not even just another high definition video format. This was HDV, the first HD video format specifically designed to provide HD access for the masses. Suddenly, there was an HD format that could produce incredible images with equipment that cost a fraction of the price of traditional HD camcorders.

HD is no longer the exclusive domain of the elite; it's now within reach of wedding videographers, educational institutions, even nonprofessional video enthusiasts.

You are probably reading this book because HDV has peaked your interest or you have already made an investment in the format. We'd like to think this book can serve as a guide for video beginners or professionals who are new to HDV. For those of you new to video production, jumping into HDV means jumping over standard definition and developing your skills in what will inevitably become the production norm over the next few years. For video veterans who are used to SD productions, you have the new challenges of a wider aspect ratio and improved resolution, among others. We found it best that you treat an HDV camcorder more like a film camera in terms of lighting and shooting, which means a re-education of sorts with regard to framing and camera movement.

It was also our desire not to spend too much time in this book discussing the overly technical aspects of HDV. There are excellent books out there on this topic. We would rather educate or enlighten you on what cameras are available, how best to utilize them, and what options you have in editing.

The first three chapters provide a solid foundation for your HDV education. We've provided a discussion of HD, complete with historical perspective and HDV-specific information. We delve into some business considerations, and even provide a primer on digital video technology.

Beginning with Chapter 4, however, the discussion turns to the cameras themselves, what they do best, and how you can make them work best for you. Even in this first wave of HDV camcorders, it is apparent that one size does not fit all. With a relatively small number of professional HDV camcorders on the market, we felt it was important to provide detailed information on your available options—though we'd like to think our discussion moves beyond simple product literature regurgitation.

As of this writing, all of the cameras mentioned (except one) are still in production or under development by manufacturers. Unfortunately, product offerings change regularly in this industry. It's simply not possible for a book like this to remain on the cutting edge of technology for very long, but the production techniques will not change, and most camera features will either remain or be enhanced on future models. In other words, we hope this will be a valuable resource for you even after the specific camcorders in the book have been upgraded or replaced.

After you shoot your first few minutes with an HDV camcorder, we think you won't want to retreat to SD shooting again. In the past, the quality of HD imagery has been compared to looking out a window. Today, HDV affords videographers at every level the opportunity to create their own windows to the world. Whether you are shooting an independent feature or a local TV commercial, you are only limited by your imagination.

Welcome to the world of HDV.

Acknowledgments

Chuck Gloman

I would like to thank all of the millions, I mean dozens of people who helped make this book possible for me. This list is not in any order of preference, importance, stature, or IQ, but all of these fine individuals deserve credit—and you should always give credit where credit is due, especially if a big guy named Knuckles says you "owe" him.

Thanks go out to Elinor Actipis and Becky Golden-Harrell from Focal Press for their help and enthusiasm with the book; Tim Kolb, our illustrious and very knowledgeable tech editor, who made sure we were not spouting gibberish; my students at DeSales University, who posed for pictures for this book; my family who kept asking, "Is it finished yet?" (I assume they were talking about the book); my co-author Mark J. Pescatore, who helped considerably in the writing stages, meeting deadlines, and whose friendship I value even though he is my boss at *Government Video*; companies such as Sony, JVC, Canon, and others who let me evaluate their latest HDV equipment for *Government Video*, *Videography*, and this book; my fan club (all right, I don't have one yet, but there has to be one or two of you out there), who look forward to my next book; and for being so blessed with the talent and experience I have gained from this ever changing, wonderful field we know as video.

Mark J. Pescatore, Ph.D.

First and foremost, I have to thank Chuck for inviting me to join him on this whirlwind experience. Whether it was an act of friendship, kissing up, or self-preservation in the face of impossible deadlines, I am grateful. And tired.

I also need to thank some industry professionals who really came through for us with photos, technical insight, and legal stuff: Geoff Coalter, Deborah Szajngarten, and Joseph Bogacz at Canon; Jose Rosado at Ikegami; Brian McKernan at Marcomm Group; Dave Walton and Craig Yanagi at JVC; Pat Lamb, Jim Wickizer, and Phil Livingston at Panasonic; Candace Vadnais at PFS Marketwyse; Tom Di Nome and Hugo Gaggioni at Sony; and Denise Williams and John Naylor at Thomson Grass Valley. Special thanks to my bosses at CMP Entertainment Media, who authorized and encouraged this moonlighting effort, and to my family and friends for their continued support of my efforts to "make TV" for a living in one form or another.

About the Authors

Chuck Gloman has been actively working in the field since 1980 when he graduated from the Pennsylvania State University with a B.A. in film. While pursuing a master's degree at the same school, he worked a variety of jobs in the industry, gaining valuable experience (and little money).

With M.A. in hand, he found a new field in its infancy called *video*. After selling his master's thesis film, *The Butler Did It,* to HBO and Cinemax (where it remained for nine years), he worked for PBS before landing a job as an instructional designer and scriptwriter for a cutting-edge community college. Creating, shooting, and editing interactive videotapes displayed on an Apple II, he was hurled into the video industry and computer technology. After a three-year stint in Virginia working as a director shooting interactive videodiscs for the U.S. Armed Services and the government (traveling the country and visiting almost every base and post in the United States), he moved to Pennsylvania and became a producer, creating videodiscs for Federal Express, IBM, Turner Network, Simon & Schuster, the Singapore Ministry of Defense, the U.S. Department of Defense, and Ford Motor Company.

In the mid-1990s he was creative services director at an NBC affiliate. There he wrote and directed more than 600 television commercials. Moving back to corporate videos in the late 1990s, he handled most of Armstrong World Industries' video presentations (over 200) and shot how-to installation videos for Lowe's. Still active in the freelance market, he moved out on his own in 2001 as a producer/director of photography, creating over 100 documentaries, 200 commercials, and dozens of corporate videos for clients such as: ESPN, FOX Television, Rite Aid, Weis, PAX Network, Coca-Cola, FEMA, UGI, March of Dimes, Fuji Corporation, the History Channel, and Lockheed Martin.

His love of lighting led him into education, as adjunct faculty to Bradley Academy for the Performing Arts, where he taught production and lighting courses. Currently, he is a full-time member of the faculty at DeSales University, where he teaches TV/film courses.

Chuck is also a contributing editor to *Videography* and *Government Video* magazines, and has been working with co-author Mark J. Pescatore at *Government Video* since 2001. In addition to the above magazines, he has written for: *TV Technology;, Television Broadcast; Philly Tech; Mix; Sound and Video Contractor; Digital Cinema; Miata; 911 Magazine; Erosion Control; Sports TV Production; Systems Contractor News;* and *Motor Trend Classic*. He has also published the following books: *Placing Shadows: Lighting Techniques for Video Production, 2nd Edition* (Burlington, MA: Focal Press 2000); *Horror Stories: Never Leave Your Imagination Alone* (eNovel, 2001); *No Budget Digital Filmmaking* (McGraw-Hill, 2002); *303 Digital Filmmaking Solutions* (McGraw-Hill, 2003); *202 Digital Photography Solutions* (McGraw-Hill, 2003); *Placing Shadows: Lighting Techniques for Video Production, 3rd Edition* (Focal Press, 2005); and *Basic Scenic Design and Lighting* (Focal Press, 2006).

Mark J. Pescatore, Ph.D., has been the editor of *Government Video* magazine since 2000, and has been reporting on the video industry since 1994. He has also served as the executive conference chair for the annual Government Video & Technology Expo in Washington, D.C. since 2002.

In 2003 and 2004, he was the co-instructor for the JVC-sponsored HDV Roadshow, which introduced the new format to video professionals in cities across the United States.

His articles have appeared in a number of other magazines, including *Videography*, *Television Broadcast*, and *Systems Contractor News*. He has also been published in academic journals, including the *Journal of Broadcast and Electronic Media* and *Feedback*, and has presented his academic research at conferences of the Broadcast Education Association and the Association for Education in Journalism and Mass Communication. Mark has contributed to *The Guide to Digital Television* (Miller Freeman PSN, Inc., 1998); *Encyclopedia of Communication and Information* (Macmillan Reference USA, 2001); and *Digital Television: DTV and the Consumer* (Blackwell Publishing Professional, 2004). In addition, he served as co-editor on the second and third editions of *The Guide to Digital Television* (Miller Freeman PSN, Inc., 1999 and 2000).

As program manager for a community programming cable channel in the mid-1990s, Mark was responsible for hundreds of productions, from a live morning show to local high school sports coverage. Limited resources meant that Mark was a hands-on manager, often serving as writer, director, editor, videographer, and even talent for various shows, news packages, and PSAs. He has also taught more than a dozen college courses, including television production, news writing, and public speaking. Mark earned his doctorate in mass communication from the University of North Carolina at Chapel Hill, and has a master's degree in telecommunication and film from The University of Alabama, a bachelor's degree in communication from Florida Atlantic University, and an associate's degree in mass communication from Broward Community College.

CHAPTER 1

A History of High Definition

HDV® was not the first high definition video format introduced, nor is it likely to be the last. However, since the announcement of the format in 2003, HDV has been enthusiastically accepted by professional videographers, independent filmmakers, local broadcast news operations, national network television programs, and proud parents on graduation day. Clearly this affordable acquisition option—supported by a growing supply of camcorders, editing solutions, and ancillary equipment—is making an impact in the video industry.

But we're getting ahead of ourselves.

Before we dissect the HDV format, it's important to put HDV in perspective. HDV has become so popular because it brings true HD acquisition to consumers and professionals with smaller budgets. The reason for the interest in low-cost HD is because HDTV sets continue to set record sales. The reason why HDTV sets have become so popular is because there is a large selection of HD programs on television. And the reason why there is so much HD on TV is because of a federally mandated change from the U.S. television broadcast transmission standard that has been in place since the 1950s to digital television (DTV), a change that gives stations the ability to broadcast HD programming and a lot more.

This first chapter provides a general overview of the changes in U.S. broadcast policy. Once we have established a timeline, it will be time to debunk some of the common myths and misinformation surrounding HDTV. We will even take a look at the consumer HD marketplace, and begin to explore how HDV fits into this new world of higher definition. First, however, we really need to define "HD," because it's not as straightforward as you might think.

High Definition Defined

In the United States, standard definition refers to the resolution of the broadcast standard developed by the National Television Systems Committee (NTSC), which was adopted by the FCC in 1953. It has 525 horizontal scanning lines of information, and 480 of these lines—called "effective" scanning lines—are used to create a *frame*, or image, on your television. The other lines are called the vertical blanking interval (VBI), and are used to transmit additional data, such as closed captioning. Other countries use the PAL and SECAM broadcast systems, with 625 scanning lines and 576 effective lines. In this book, when we refer to standard definition, or SD, we mean 480i (we'll get to the "i" in a moment).

High definition, in contrast, offers many more lines of resolution. However, there are two distinct HD systems. The first offers 1,080 lines of resolution, while the second offers 720 lines. Even to a non-engineer, the numbers tell the story—either 720 or 1,080 is more than 480. More lines means more resolution. True, but there are other reasons why HD provides a better viewing experience than SD. Television pictures are built from small picture elements, or pixels. Both NTSC and PAL have 720 active horizontal pixels per line. HD, however, has many more. A 720-line system has 1,280 pixels per line, while a 1080-line system can offer 1,440 or 1,920 pixels per line.

Why so many more pixels? HD also features a wider *aspect ratio* than SD. The aspect ratio is the ratio of the width of the screen to the height of the screen. The HD aspect ratio is 16:9, which more closely resembles the widescreen aspect ratio of modern motion pictures shown in movie theatres. In SD, the aspect ratio is almost always 4:3. We say "almost" because there have been a number of SD camcorders that produce 16:9 pictures, which mimic the aspect ratio of HD but don't equal its resolution. You'll get much more detail about aspect ratio in Chapter 5. For now, when we refer to SD images, we are talking 4:3, while HD images are widescreen or 16:9. **Figure 1.1A** and **1.1B** illustrates the difference between HD and SD.

Figure 1.1A High definition images have more resolution and a wider aspect ratio than standard definition.

Figure 1.1B Standard definition looks good, but there's no comparison to HD.

So, if more lines means more resolution, then 1080-line HD has more reso-lution than 720-line HD, right? Technically, 1080-line HD has more pixels per line and has more effective scanning lines. However, these systems have different ways of "building" television pictures, which has been the cause of much debate in the television industry. This is where we talk about the "i" and another lower-case letter, "p."

The "i" stands for *interlaced scanning*. Basically, one frame of video is di-vided into two fields, one with all the even lines of resolution, the other with the odd lines of resolution. The two fields are then combined (or interlaced) together to form a complete picture. See **Figure 1.2**.

Figure 1.2 An interlaced scanning system separates a video frame into two fields and combines them to form a complete picture.

Interlaced scanning was a rather clever way of condensing (or compressing) the NTSC signal for transmission. As you will learn in Chapter 3, your eyes can be easily fooled; after all, video is nothing more than a series of still images. A *frame rate* of 30 frames per second (fps) using an interlaced signal (60 fields) is fast enough to create the illusion of motion. (PAL is an interlaced system with a frame rate of 25 fps, which is why British programming seems to have a slight flicker to U.S. viewers.)

Interlaced technology is still in use today, and is part of the 1080-line system. That's why it's called 1080i. Computers use a different method of building an image, which is the technology incorporated into the 720-line format. In a *progressive scanning* or "p" system, the entire frame is scanned consecutively from top to bottom without dividing the frame into two separate fields. See **Figure 1.3**.

Figure 1.3 The complete frame of video is scanned as one complete image in a progressive scanning system.

Now let's get back to the resolution argument, because it provides an ideal segue into discussing the advantages and disadvantages of both systems. The 1080i format may seem like it has more lines of resolution, but each frame is actually a combination of two fields with 540 lines each. As a result, your eyes technically only see 540 lines at a time. The 720p system, however, does not break up its frames into separate fields, so it has 720 lines of resolution in every frame. But let us not forget that the 1080i system has more horizontal pixels per line.

Yes, engineers have been fighting over the supremacy of one format over another for years with an almost fanatic fervor. Where does it end? The truth is that while both 1080i and 720p systems can create incredible HD imagery, there are advantages and disadvantages to both. With 1080i, you've got a system that your eyes are used to seeing, and do not be quick to discount the intrinsic appeal of familiarity. Plus, because its frames are separated into fields, it actually uses less *bandwidth* to transmit, something that will become more important when we talk about DTV broadcast options. That said, the interlaced scanning system can sometimes cause *artifacts*, or unwanted picture elements.

Supporters of 720p make strong arguments as well. Because each picture is a complete frame, it tends to handle motion better, making it an ideal fit for sports and other high-action programming. Also, as the video and computer worlds continue to converge at the professional and consumer levels, it makes sense that both would share the same display system. However, you can't fool your eyes all the time, and watching 720p at 30 fps will cause noticeable flicker. As a result, you need to transmit 60 frames per second, and those full frames of information take much more bandwidth during transmission than 1080i.

So which format is better, 720p or 1080i? It depends on who you ask. Both formats have their share of supporters. At the network television level, for example, ABC and FOX® both opted for 720p, while CBS and NBC chose 1080i. To a degree, it comes down to personal preference. For the record, the HDV format supports 720p and 1080i recording, though not every HDV camcorder can record in both. Now that you know what high definition is, it will be easier to explain why its popularity continues to increase.

Points of Interest

- High definition images have more lines of resolution and more pixels per line than standard definition images.

- Most SD formats have a 4:3 aspect ratio, while HD always has a 16:9 image.

- There are two ways to build a video frame, interlaced scanning and progressive scanning. Each method has advantages and disadvantages.

The DTV Transition

Originally, it was a black-and-white world, at least on TV. The first television broadcast standard in the United States was established by the NTSC in 1941 and remained in effect for more than a decade. In the New York World's Fair of 1939, the public was introduced to television for the very first time. It took until 1941 to develop the "standard." Later, the committee modified its standard so it could transmit color images.

The NTSC color TV standard was adopted by the Federal Communications Commission (FCC) in 1953 and has been the way U.S. viewers have been receiving over-the-air television signals for more than 50 years. Soon, however, this analog technology will be replaced by more advanced digital transmissions that offer the promise of improved picture quality and expanded services. (We'll get into the differences between analog and digital in more detail in Chapter 3.) For the past few years, the United States has been involved in a DTV transition, and it is this transition that has sparked increased interest in high definition production.

The FCC's first inquiry into advanced television (ATV) services was in 1987, when 58 broadcast organizations jointly petitioned the FCC to explore the potential impact of ATV technologies on existing broadcast service. That same year, the Advisory Committee on Advanced Television Service (ACATS) was established by the FCC to make recommendations concerning ATV technical and economic issues. Meanwhile, all-digital ATV systems were developed, prompting officials to replace ATV with another acronym. DTV was born.

As broadcasters, manufacturers, and cable television system operators began working on various DTV technologies and standards, there was always one important consideration for implementation: There could be no disruption of service to the public while stations transitioned to digital transmission. But a television station could not broadcast a digital signal on the same frequency as its existing analog signal, so how could it maintain its analog signal and begin broadcasting digitally? It was decided that a separate channel would be assigned to each broadcaster for its DTV signal using a different part of the broadcast spectrum. Once the DTV transition was complete, broadcasters would be required to surrender their NTSC frequencies, so they could be used for other services.

By February 1993, the FCC was considering four different digital systems, but none were recommended by ACATS. A few months later, seven companies and institutions that had worked on the rejected digital systems decided to work together. This "Grand Alliance" developed a new DTV system that was recommended to the FCC in late 1995 by the Advanced Television Systems Committee (ATSC), an organization that had been formed to establish DTV standards.

On December 27, 1996, the FCC adopted a modified version of this DTV standard in its Fourth Report and Order. With the standard in place, the FCC moved quickly to get the transition started. It released the Fifth Report and Order on April 21, 1997, a document that outlined the rules and services policies for the DTV transition. It included an aggressive eight-year strategy in which to complete the DTV transition, including a market-staggered approach to adoption.

About the ATSC

The Advanced Television Systems Committee is a nonprofit organization that was established in 1982 to develop voluntary standards for DTV. It was created by the member organizations of the Joint Committee on Intersociety Coordination (JCIC), which included the Electronic Industries Association (EIA), the Institute of Electrical and Electronic Engineers (IEEE), the National Association of Broadcasters (NAB), the National Cable Television Association (NCTA), and the Society of Motion Picture and Television Engineers (SMPTE). It now boasts a membership of about 140 members, including companies from a variety of communications industries. The FCC adopted a modified version of its DTV standard for U.S. broadcasters in 1996. Since then, the ATSC's DTV standard has also been adopted by Canada, South Korea, Argentina, and Mexico.

All stations in the top 10 markets affiliated with the major networks (ABC, CBS, FOX, and NBC) were required to be broadcasting a digital signal by May 1, 1999. Six months later, all major network affiliates in the top 30 markets were required to follow suit. All other commercial stations, including independent stations and UPN, WB, and PAX affiliates, had until May 1, 2002, to begin digital transmissions, while noncommercial stations, such as PBS member stations, were required to have their digital signals on the air by May 1, 2003. Hundreds of commercial and noncommercial stations failed to meet their deadlines and had to file for extensions (and most had to file for additional extensions).

As shown in **Table 1.1**, more than 90 percent of DTV stations were on the air as of March 2006, but there were still more than 150 stations not broadcasting digitally. Plus, more than 40 percent of stations were operating under Special Temporary Authorities (STAs), which do not operate at full power. Originally, broadcasters were supposed to surrender their analog frequencies in 2006, but that date proved unrealistic as the transition moved slower than anticipated by lawmakers. As a result, the deadline for the end of the digital transition was pushed to February 2009.

Table 1.1 DTV stations authorized to be on the air
March 24, 2006

Category	Number of DTV Stations on the Air	Number of DTV Channels	Percentage on the Air	With Licensed Facility or Program Tests	WITH STAs
Top 30 Market Network Affiliates	119	119	100%	110	9
Other Commercial Stations*	1,109	1,230	90.2%	534	575
Noncommercial Educational**	338	373	90.6%	243	95
Total	1,566	1,722***	90.9%	887	679

* May 1, 2002 Build-out deadline
** May 1, 2003 Build-out deadline
*** Includes single-channel DTV operations

This table shows the progress of the DTV transition. Three years after all stations were required to be broadcasting DTV signals, more than 150 authorized DTV channels were still not on the air. Source: FCC.

While broadcasters scrambled for DTV equipment, and manufacturers scrambled to meet the demands for new transmitters and towers, the early years of the DTV transition were marked by a number of DTV "firsts." CBS affiliate WRAL-HD in Raleigh, North Carolina, signed on the first commercial experimental HDTV signal on July 23, 1996. The following year, on November 28, 1997, ABC affiliate KITV in Honolulu, Hawaii, began broadcasting the first commercial DTV signal. Its satellite station, KHVO in Hilo, also received the first FCC DTV construction permit.

Figure 1.4 NASA's 1998 Space Shuttle Mission with 77-year-old crew member U.S. Senator John Glenn was the first national HDTV broadcast.

Figure 1.5 High definition programming is no longer a novelty for many networks. In 2005, for example, ESPN went on location to Jacksonville, Florida, for pre-game coverage of the Super Bowl in HD.

The first national HDTV broadcast provided coverage of the October 29, 1998, Space Shuttle Mission STS-95, notable for its 77-year-old crew member, U.S. Senator John Glenn. Three days later, 26 volunteer stations, as well as several early adopters, began broadcasting regular digital signals, although very few DTV sets had been sold. HBO® launched the first HD pay channel in March 6, 1999, and on April 26, 1999, *The Tonight Show with Jay Leno* debuted as the first regularly scheduled HD show. Super Bowl® XXXIV, on January 30, 2000, became the first Super Bowl to get the HD broadcast treatment, culminating an entire season of HD coverage on ABC's *Monday Night Football*® (see **Figure 1.4**).

These days, the novelty of HDTV "firsts" is long gone. HD programming has become the norm for broadcast network primetime programming. While some news programs and reality shows are still produced in SD, almost all scripted situation comedies and dramas are now available in HD. Some cable networks, such as TNT®, A&E®, and ESPN®, offer HD channels, as do a number of subscription movie channels, including HBO and Showtime®. There are also channels available exclusively in HD, such as HDNet and HDNet Movies (see **Figure 1.5**).

Sports programming also continues to expand its HD offerings. There is still a mix of SD and HD coverage, but more and more professional and even college-level contests are getting the HD treatment. According to a survey by the Consumer Electronics Association (CEA), sports fans are a driving force in HD sales. Sports programming was cited as the primary reason for an HDTV purchase by almost half of surveyed owners.

Points of Interest

- DTV was developed to provide improved picture quality and services for over-the-air viewers.

- The DTV standard was adopted by the FCC in 1996.

- While the DTV transition has progressed slower than the FCC's original timeline, analog television is scheduled to be shut down in the United States in February 2009.

DTV Broadcast Options

The U.S. DTV broadcast standard was established in 1996, the rules for the DTV transition were adopted in 1997, and DTV sets have been available in retail stores since 1998. Still, confusion about the new era of television lingers. Blame it on a number of factors—from a crop of confusing new terms and acronyms to poor efforts at consumer education—but the fact remains that the DTV transition has not gone as smoothly as it could have.

Arguably the largest stumbling block for consumers is using the terms "DTV" and "HDTV" interchangeably. They are not one and the same. HDTV is one of several broadcast options available to DTV broadcasters. There is no FCC mandate for HDTV, which means broadcast stations are not required to transmit high definition programs. As more viewers invest in HDTVs and expect to see HD programming, you could argue that at some point (in the not-too-distant future) a broadcast station that fails to provide HD could wind up losing large portions of its audience. But the decision to go HD is a business decision for broadcasters, not a government mandate.

Adding to the confusion is that all DTV images look better than analog TV; after all, there's no reason to change a well-established broadcast standard for television images that are only as good as or possibly worse than current images. The ATSC broadcast standard includes 18 different formats for DTV transmission. As shown in **Table 1.2**, some are SD, others are HD. (Now you know why there are 1080i and 720p HD options—because both are acceptable DTV transmission standards.) So, DTV is an improvement over analog TV, but not all DTV images are HD images.

Table 1.2 ATSC Table 3 Formats for DTV Transmission (interlaced, progressive).

Vertical Size Value (Active)	Horizontal Size Value (Active)	Aspect Ratio Information	Frame Rate and Scan
(HD) 1,080	1,920	16:9 (square pixel)	24p, 30p, 30i
(HD) 720	1,280	16:9 (square pixel)	24p, 30p, 60p
(SD) 480	704	4:3 (nonsquare pixel)	24p, 30p, 30i, 60p
(SD) 480	704	16:9 (nonsquare pixel)	24p, 30p, 30i, 60p
(SD) 480	640	4:3 (square pixel)	24p, 30p, 30i, 60p

The ATSC broadcast standard adopted by the FCC in 1996 includes 18 different formats for DTV transmission.

Based on the ATSC Table 3 chart, there are five main characteristics of a digital video format: the number of active lines per picture, the number of active pixels per line, aspect ratio, frame rate, and method of scanning (interlaced or progressive). Let's take a closer look at the chart to make sure all its nuances are explained. You're already familiar with active vertical and horizontal values, as well as differences in aspect ratios. But what are square or nonsquare pixels? Actually a square pixel is simply one that has equal height and width. Traditionally used for computer graphics, square pixels are preferred in today's digital environment because they tend to create fewer artifacts. NTSC pixels are slightly taller than they are wide, so they are nonsquare pixels. The PAL standard also uses nonsquare pixels, but they are slightly wider than they are tall.

The last column requires additional explaining as well. You already know about interlaced and progressive scanning, but there are a number of frame rate choices. Why so many? The idea was to give broadcasters a variety of acceptable transmission formats, and let market forces decide which formats would be used the most. As expected, video professionals have gravitated toward only a few of the formats, including the three we have previously discussed, 480i, 1080i, and 720p, which could technically be expressed as 480i/30, 1080i/30, and 720p/60. Formats and frame rates can be written in a variety of ways, but for the sake of simplicity, we'll only use this method.

Let's revisit the 720p versus 1080i argument for a moment. Honestly, a 1080p/60 transmission format would probably quiet the debate between 720p and 1080i once and for all, as it would have the most lines of resolution and progressive scanning. (It is already used as a production format.) As you can see, however, 1080p/60 is not an ATSC DTV transmission format. Why? To answer that, we have to revisit the issue of bandwidth.

Unlike an analog broadcast signal, which can only broadcast one channel at a time, a digital broadcast signal can carry a variety of information. A digital signal is composed of data, and its bandwidth represents the amount of data that a DTV channel can transmit. The ATSC DTV bandwidth can handle about 19.39 megabits per second (Mbps) of data, which is more than enough to provide a number of options for broadcasters, though not quite big enough to handle 1080p/60. Let's explore some of the ways broadcasters can use their bandwidth.

Hungry? Imagine a broadcaster's DTV options are similar to your options in a cafeteria. You get one plate (sorry, no seconds). You can fill that plate with a number of different choices from the menu, but you can't pile different kinds of food on top of each other and you can't let your food choices spill over the sides of the plate. Scrambled and overflowing signals give broadcasters a very bad case of indigestion, also known as transmission errors and interference.

So, how will you fill your plate? One option is high definition. It's a big, thick, juicy steak. The tastiest, most tempting item in the cafeteria. On television, HD is the undisputed prime cut, with spectacular, clear images that have often been compared to looking out a window. And once you get a taste for it, everything else in the cafeteria sort of loses a bit of its flavor. The problem with HD is that it takes up a very big part of your plate. In other words, it takes a lot of bandwidth to transmit HD, so it limits your other choices.

Perhaps you're one of those eaters that likes to get the same thing every time, a cheeseburger. It might not be as delicious as the steak, but it is pretty tasty and it will satisfy your hunger. Broadcasters have the option of simply transmitting the same standard definition images they have been showing in the past. While not HD, they will look better than current SD signals. Plus, a cheeseburger takes up a lot less room on your plate (we will not get into cholesterol).

Maybe you have a very big appetite and one cheeseburger will just not be enough to stop your stomach from grumbling. So you add a chicken sandwich to your plate. And some lasagna. And a side salad. It is one of the more intriguing options on the menu available to broadcasters and it is called *multicasting*. Because the DTV signal is data, the bandwidth can be divided in a number of ways. In fact, it can be used to transmit two or more distinct program streams simultaneously. (You would not transmit the same program stream twice, which is why you did not fill your plate with cheeseburgers.)

DTV bandwidth can actually support up to four SD channels without a problem. In a multicasting environment, the primary channel would be called, for example, 12-1, while the secondary channels would be listed as 12-2, 12-3, and 12-4. You can even fit one HD signal and a couple of SD signals on your plate, so you can have your steak with a couple of side dishes.

What do broadcasters do with these additional channels? Some have elected to use a secondary channel for additional services, such as 24-hour local weather. Others lease those channels to other program providers. PBS is committed to the promise of multicasting technology, as it provides additional outlets for its programming (and because PBS is non-commercial in nature, it does not have to worry about ratings or dividing its audience). So, one local PBS member station can dedicate one subchannel just to children's programming and another to college courses, while still providing an HD feed of national programming.

Finally, you should take a look at the dessert tray. Depending on what you have already selected, you might have just enough room on your plate for a slice of pie. For broadcasters, that extra space on the tray can be used for *datacasting*, which delivers nonbroadcast material to televisions and computers. It can include any kind of data, from text and graphics to audio and video, and the data can be used for program guides, education materials that augment broadcast content, even emergency information. Datacasting could eventually be a revenue stream for broadcasters. Sweet.

Points of Interest

- Not all DTV images are high definition.

- The ATSC DTV transmission standard provides broadcasters with 18 acceptable formats.

- DTV broadcasters can use their bandwidth to provide a variety of options, including high definition, multiple channels of programming, and data services.

DTV and Consumers

So, what does the DTV transition mean to consumers? First, understand that DTV has become mainstream: HDTV is available at a Wal-Mart® near you. It is no longer the high-tech toy of the early adopter; it is conveniently located between the socks and automotive accessories. While it offers the promise of high definition programming and additional services, DTV also means a fundamental change in the way television signals are broadcast. As a result, consumers are faced with new equipment purchases, new options from cable and satellite service providers, and a bewildering new batch of technological terminology.

One of the reasons for consumer confusion is the number of DTV choices available. Just as not every DTV signal is an HD signal, not every DTV set is an HDTV set. Some models can only display SD resolution (HD material is downconverted). Other sets are classified as enhanced definition televisions (EDTVs), which provide a 480p picture that is a big improvement over 480i but still not true HD. There are even DTV sets (including some HDTVs) that have the old 4:3 aspect ratio instead of the newer 16:9.

Plus, there is also a variety of form factors. DTV sets are available in traditional CRT models, as well as LCD flat screens, plasma flat screens, and large-screen displays that incorporate any number of projection technologies. Since DTV sets became available in August 1998, sales have shown steady and promising growth. According to the CEA, there were 121,225 factory-to-dealer DTV sales in 1999. Six years later, more than 12 million units were sold in 2005, with HD products accounting for 85 percent of sales.

To keep consumer electronics manufacturers on track with the DTV transition, the FCC established a phased-in DTV tuner requirement, whereby receivers in new TVs were required to receive DTV signals. The plan began with larger, more expensive sets, with the idea that digital tuner prices would become lower as the quantity of tuners increased. As a result, smaller and less expensive sets would not shoulder the full impact of the new tuner requirement, and prices could be kept reasonable.

The requirement began in July 2004, when manufacturers were required to equip half of TV sets 36 inches and larger with DTV tuners. By July 2005, all large sets were required to include DTV tuners, as well as 50 percent of mid-size sets (25–35 inches). All new mid-size sets were require to comply by March 2006, with all new TV receivers of any size to include a DTV tuner as of March 2007. Originally, the DTV tuner requirement was not applied to televisions that were less than 13 inches in size. However, in the aftermath of several hurricanes that devastated parts of the United States in 2004 and 2005, the FCC realized the value of portable, often battery-powered televisions in times of emergency and amended its requirements. Of course, some manufacturers have side-stepped the requirement by offering "monitors" of various sizes with no tuner in them at all, requiring consumers to rely on cable, satellite, or separate receivers to receive programming.

While DTV tuners will be the norm for all new televisions by 2007, millions of analog TVs are still being sold in the United States, millions of analog TVs are in storage waiting to be sold, and millions of analog TVs are already in use. Are all these televisions going to be obsolete in 2009? Well, yes. And no.

Remember that a DTV signal is a data stream. An analog TV is not designed to decode the data and turn it into a TV picture. In fact, it is not even designed to receive the digital signals because it is "looking" for channels in a different part of the broadcast spectrum. Once the DTV transition is complete and the NTSC frequencies have been surrendered by broadcasters, today's analog TVs will not be able to receive over-the-air television transmissions without help.

Enter the set-top box (STB). An external DTV tuner can be connected to an analog television so it can receive over-the-air DTV signals. (Thankfully, the same antennas that work for analog TV also work for DTV.) You will not see HD pictures on an SD set—analog televisions are still limited to their existing resolutions, so HD programs will be downconverted through the STB into SD images. The STB cannot enhance the picture quality of an existing set; all it can do is decode the incoming digital information and convert it to analog so it can be seen on an old-fashioned TV. By the time STBs are required accessories, experts expect them to be priced between $50 and $100.

Not all U.S. television households receive their programming over the air. According to Nielsen Media Research™, there were approximately 110 million U.S. television households as of January 2006, with cable serving more than 73 million of them. Needless to say, cable industry cooperation was critical to the success of the DTV transition. While broadcasters and cable companies have had their share of disagreements over the DTV transition (and other matters), the cable industry's 10 largest operators endorsed a voluntary call to action by FCC chairman Michael Powell in 2002 to speed the DTV transition. According to the National Cable & Telecommunications Association (NCTA), 96 million U.S. households were passed by at least one cable system with HDTV service as of September 2005. There were also 681 unique DTV broadcast signals being carried by local cable systems, compared to just 92 in January 2003.

As established by the Cable Act of 1992, local broadcasters have the option of requiring local cable operators to carry their channel. However, in 2005, the FCC determined this "must carry" legislation did not require cable operators to carry a broadcaster's analog and digital signals. In addition, the FCC ruled that must carry does not apply to multiple broadcast streams. In other words, must carry only applies to the "primary video" of a broadcast station, not additional channels broadcast through multicasting. Cable systems are, of course, free to negotiate retransmission of additional signals with broadcasters.

Cable systems have limited bandwidth (known in the industry as shelf space) for channels; however, as the FCC reported in 2004, the industry has begun its own migration to digital technology to provide more channels and services to subscribers. HD channels are positioned on a digital cable tier, which generally requires customers to lease a special STB and pay an additional monthly charge. However, many of the new DTV sets are "digital cable ready," meaning they feature a plug-and-play access card, also known as a CableCARD™, so they can access digital cable channels without using a separate STB. The plug-and-play standards were established in December 2002 through an agreement between major consumer electronics companies and cable multiple system operators (MSOs). The cable industry had deployed more than 27,000 CableCARDs by February 2005, according to the NCTA.

Another option for consumers is satellite TV, also known as Direct-to-Home Satellite Service. It uses DBS satellites to transmit digital signals to small DBS dish antennas installed at the home, and then the signals are decoded by an STB. The industry has seen significant growth in the United States since it was introduced in 1994, with DirecTV® and EchoStar's DISH® Network among the more popular programming providers. According to Media Business Group, an independent media research firm, there were more than 27 million DBS subscribers in 2005.

DBS systems already offer a number of HDTV channel choices, though most local channels are offered via satellite in SD. However, some satellite receivers feature an integrated DTV tuner. When combined with an antenna, you can tune in local DTV channels and watch local HD content on your HDTV. Satellite companies continue to upgrade their receiver and compression technologies, so it is not unrealistic to think that local HD channels could eventually become part of the satellite channel offerings.

As illustrated, HDV is only one part of the high definition story. And while HDV has brought affordable HD to consumers and professionals alike, its popularity is, at least in part, a result of a much larger adoption of HD in the marketplace. Now that you have some perspective, Chapter 2 will explore some of the misconceptions regarding HD and how HDV should factor into your video production business plan.

Points of Interest

- DTV set sales have steadily increased since they were introduced in 1998, with HDTVs accounting for the vast majority of sales.

- While analog TVs will be obsolete when the DTV transition is complete, set-top boxes will allow them to receive and convert DTV signals.

- Consumers can receive HD content through over-the-air DTV, most cable operators, and DBS satellite program providers.

CHAPTER 2

The HDV Revolution

"Good enough." Those are two of the most important words in professional video. Whether you shoot weddings, city commission meetings, or national primetime programming, there is a level of quality you would like to achieve and a level of quality that you must accept. If you are fortunate, those two levels are pretty close to each other. Usually, however, compromises must be made, though some concessions turn out to be better than expected.

It worked for DV. After all, lowly DV formats like Sony DVCAM® and Panasonic® DVCPRO™ were not really supposed to have "real" professional applications. Maybe it was "good enough" for corporate video, but surely it was not up to standard for broadcast television, right? Wrong.

A handful of local television stations pride themselves on being pioneers, adopting cutting-edge technologies and leading the DTV revolution. Most, however, do not. Local television news operations have a reputation for being, shall we say, thrifty. They would use masking tape instead of videotape if they could figure out a way to make it record pictures and sound. These stations rely on their news broadcasts for profits, so to maximize revenue, management works to minimize expenses.

When digital video formats like Sony DVCAM and Panasonic DVCPRO hit the market, there was an almost universal declaration of "good enough" heard throughout local news, as stations began replacing their aging Betacam® SP camcorders with newer, less expensive units. Except, of course, for the stations that maintained that their Betacam SP camcorders were "good enough" to last another five years.

That same "good enough" mentality may very well carry over to HDV. As high definition becomes more and more expected by television viewers, there will be pressure for newsrooms and other operations to upgrade to HD. Undoubtedly, HDV will be among the HD options discussed, as it is far less expensive than other established HD formats.

Some stations have already made the jump. KRON in San Francisco, California, for example, has purchased more than 50 Sony HVR-Z1U camcorders. According to chief engineer Craig Porter, the station has a group of employees that serve as reporter, videographer, and editor. Recruited from existing photographers and reporters, these "video journalists" or "one-man bands" load up a Z1 camcorder, Panasonic Toughbook® laptop with Canopus® EDIUS® nonlinear editing software, wireless mics, and a lightweight tripod into a compact car—and then report, shoot, and edit their own news stories. The Z1 investment has allowed the station to "jump into HD with both feet," Porter said. "The cameras have been much more reliable than I would have thought possible. Their low cost has allowed us to provide all of the production staff with their own camera."

KRON provides an ideal example of effective cost-cutting measures by news departments. The handheld Z1 lists for less than $5,000, a much less expensive alternative to traditional, shoulder-mounted electronic news-gathering (ENG) camcorders that record in SD. The smaller equipment can be easily transported in a smaller, more fuel efficient, and less expensive vehicle, as opposed to the typical news van. Plus, when one person serves in a variety of capacities for a news station, it certainly saves on personnel costs. And remember, this investment in HDV will not only save equipment and employee costs for the station in the long run, but it actually creates a high definition upgrade for its viewers.

While KRON has embraced HDV, not every news station is ready to make such a commitment. The video industry is not as simple to navigate as you might think; what works for one television station does not necessarily work for other stations or other nonbroadcast operations. As you learned in Chapter 1, the industry is loaded with jargon, acronyms, and options that are not always clear. HD has added another level of terms and conditions to the mix, and misinformation is rampant. This chapter will delve into some of the myths and misconceptions associated with HD, as well as some of the common terms you can expect to encounter. Plus, we will explore why the migration to HD (and HDV in particular) can make good business sense.

HD Misconceptions

A creative use of frame rates has fueled a major video misconception. In production, as opposed to transmission, frame rates are important because they can create a different "look" for your video. One frame rate in particular that has become popular is *24p*, because it is designed to more closely resemble the frame rate of film. In fact, the HDV specification was amended in 2006 to support 24p. Motion pictures run at 24 frames per second in the United States (25 fps in Europe).

One of the biggest fallacies in the industry today is that 24p means high definition. All 24p really means is that the footage has been shot in a progressive format at 24 frames per second. Just because a video has been shot in 24p does not mean that it has been shot in HD. Remember, frame rate is just one characteristic of a video format. There are several SD camcorders on the market that provide a 24p option, such as the Panasonic AG-DVX100B. Other interlace units, such as the Canon® XL H1, an HDV camcorder, provide a 24-frame option that basically imitates the 24p imitation of film.

Now, if you start working with 24p, you will invariably hear the term *3:2 pulldown*. In PAL systems, the 25 fps transmission rate matches the 25 fps film rate, so there's no problem with conversion. In the United States, however, because films run at 24 frames per second and U.S. television runs at 30 frames per second, you need a conversion process to transfer film to video.

With 3:2 pulldown, as shown in **Figure 2.1,** there is a little math involved, but it is not as complicated as you might think. Take two consecutive frames of film. Convert the first film frame into two video fields, then convert the second frame into three video fields. The two frames of film are on the movie screen for 1/12 of a second. The five fields of video are also on the screen for 1/12 of a second (remember, there are 60 fields per second). The timing matches over any five-frame period time. The 3:2 pulldown method works for film and for video shot in 24p, though we will address additional editing and output options in Chapter 6.

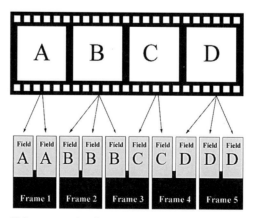

Figure 2.1 The 3:2 pulldown method is used to transfer 24 fps film to 30 fps video.

Another common mistake is to think that all 16:9 footage is HD footage. As seen in the ATSC Table 3 in Chapter 1, widescreen SD is an acceptable transmission format. Plus, as we mentioned before, there are some camcorders on the market, such as Sony's DSR-PDX10, that are native 16:9 camcorders but do not shoot HD. Again, remember the five characteristics of a video format: the number of active lines per picture, the number of active pixels per line, aspect ratio, frame rate, and method of scanning. Your footage is not HD just because it sports a wide aspect ratio.

Another easy mistake is to assume all tapeless camcorders capture in HD. The recording media does not necessarily dictate the video format. Remember, MiniDV tape was originally designed for SD acquisition, yet now it can be used to record HDV. Over the past few years, a handful of tapeless camcorders that can record in HD have been introduced (we will detail those in Chapter 7), but many use technologies originally introduced to capture SD material.

Finally, we tackle the myth of the DVD Video, a format visually superior to VHS® tapes but often given too much credit. Short for "digital versatile disc" or "digital video disc" (there never was a consensus on this), a DVD looks like a compact disc (CD) but holds more information. In fact, a DVD can hold up to 17 GB of data using two layers on both sides of the disc.

DVDs have become a dominant force in home entertainment. According to the Consumer Electronics Association, DVD players were in 81 percent of U.S. homes as of June 2005. DVD rentals overtook VHS rentals in 2003; now, most films are no longer even released on VHS, and many major retail chains have stopped selling prerecorded VHS movies.

DVD offers superior picture and audio quality over analog VHS, but it does not offer high definition. VHS only offers 240 lines of resolution, while DVD provides 480 lines of resolution. A marked improvement to be sure, but not HD, though a 480p DVD signal could be classified as enhanced definition. This means that if you are to deliver your finished HDV project on DVD, you will have to downconvert your footage.

Of course, now that we have established that DVDs are not HD, it is worth noting that new high-definition DVDs that use a different laser than current DVDs were introduced in the U.S. market in 2006. (More details are in Chapter 6.) There are competing formats, however, which could bring back a consumer format war on par with the VHS/Betamax® battle of the late 1970s. It will be interesting to see if consumers decide that 480p is "good enough," rather than invest in yet another home video format.

Points of Interest

- 24p attempts to create a film look by copying the frame rate used when motion pictures are projected at a theater.

- A 16:9 aspect ratio is not the only requirement for a format to be considered high definition.

- DVDs are not high definition, though new DVD formats that do support HD are entering the market.

Disposable SD

Randall Paris Dark has been working with HD since the mid-1980s, long before most people had even heard of HD. He is the president and co-founder of HD Vision, a Los Angeles-based production and post-production facility. He and his companies have been involved with thousands of HD projects, from stock footage to commercials to theatrically released motion pictures. In 2004, while addressing a group of HDV enthusiasts in Los Angeles, he said if you are not shooting in HD, whatever you are shooting is "disposable."

We need to put his comment in perspective. Remember, Dark has been working in HD for 20 years. He does not run a low-end shop, and his main source of income is not wedding videos or public access programming. That said, Dark's idea of disposable content deserves at least some discussion.

Whether it is a fair (or accurate) comparison or not, the DTV transition is often compared with the adoption of the NTSC color TV standard in 1956. According to the CEA, it took 10 years for color TV to achieve five percent market penetration. In other words, the vast majority of U.S. television households were still watching black-and-white televisions well into the 1960s. It was essentially a case of consumers deciding that black-and-white was "good enough" for TV.

Compare that to the adoption of DTV sets and monitors. DTVs became available in 1998. Seven years later, in 2005, DTVs had already reached more than 20 percent penetration, and the CEA expects more than half of U.S. households will have at least one DTV by 2008. While set-top boxes will allow U.S. viewers to keep using their old TVs (even black-and-white models) when the DTV transition is complete, consumers have been setting new DTV sales records every year since sets became available.

Now, bring all this information back to the idea of "disposable" programming. When was the last time you watched a black-and-white TV show or even a black-and-white movie? Unless you make a habit of watching a classic TV or movie channel, black-and-white content, particularly new content, is a rarity. This is not the 1960s, where black-and-white was "good enough;" in the 21st century, color has been the dominant viewing standard for decades. The occasional motion picture might succeed when using black-and-white as an artistic choice (1993's *Schindler's List* and 2005's *Good Night, and Good Luck,* come to mind), but if you produced television programming in black-and-white, it would not be easy to convince an audience to tune in week after week. It's no accident that programs produced for networks like the History Channel® surround black-and-white historical footage with color program elements, such as graphics, interviews, and recreations. Even compelling content is less palatable to most people if it is not presented in color.

You could make the argument, then, that black-and-white programming is "disposable" for the majority of viewers. They do not watch it because they would rather watch content in color. As we learned in Chapter 1, one of the driving forces behind DTV purchases is HD programming, and the vast majority of DTV sets sold are HDTVs. It is too early to declare that viewers will shun SD programming because they prefer HD programming, but is it really so crazy a notion? In 2013, 15 years after DTV sets became available in the United States, would it be outrageous to think that viewers would no longer be interested in SD programming? Could it become "disposable" as well?

Making a Case for HDV

Need proof that HDV has become firmly established in the video industry? There are already a number of HDV "success stories" where these low-cost camcorders are "good enough" for the national spotlight. For example, when the producers of ratings powerhouse *American Idol* decided it was time for HD, they used a combination of high-end Panasonic Varicam® HD cameras to capture on-stage performances and JVC® JY-HD10U HDV camcorders for some backstage and other behind-the-scenes footage.

Another FOX program, the critically acclaimed dramatic series *24*, has also committed to HDV on the set. According to director of photography Rodney Charters, starting with the 2006–2007 season, the show will use JVC GY-HD100U camcorders (in 24p mode) as third and fourth cameras for coverage of stunt scenes and other scenes with short shot length. "This is an additional camera," he said, " a kind of visual notebook for myself and the director to acquire those extra shots … with the ease and simplicity of a Handycam."

HDV is also making noise on the big screen. For example, director Clint Eastwood's war film, *Flags of Our Fathers*, positioned Sony Z1 camcorders in ammo boxes and used handheld Z1s as "stealth" cameras in battle sequences. For the movie *Homo Erectus*, director of photography and visual effects supervisor Scott Billups used the Canon XL H1 HDV camcorder as a second camera. He said some of the shots in the movie are not only from the XL H1 but are indistinguishable from the footage shot using a Grass Valley Viper camera, which is much more expensive and has far more demanding image specifications.

While more and more projects are being shot with HDV, it is not seen as an equal to the high-end HD cameras used by national programs or motion pictures. A common thread throughout these high-profile success stories is that HDV camcorders are at best augmenting the more expensive cameras on high-end shoots, not replacing them. On *24*, for example, HDV footage is used as a backup to the production's Panavision 35mm film cameras. And in *Flags of Our Fathers* and *Homo Erectus*, HDV camcorders were used sparingly, not as the main cameras for the shoots. For these applications, HDV footage might be ready for primetime, but not exactly ready for the spotlight.

Even if you dismiss the use of HDV by national networks and theatrically released motion pictures, and even if your video operation cannot relate to the extensive adoption of HDV by stations like KRON, it's not difficult to make a case for HDV. There are a lucky few—a very small minority—who actually produce videos for the pure artistic joy of it, with no limitations on budget and no regard for the bottom line. These people are extremely fortunate and can skip the rest of this chapter.

The rest of us have to remember that the second word in show business is "business." If you've read this far, you are probably serious about starting a career in video production or serious about building on the career you've already established. Why should you invest in HDV? Creative choices notwithstanding, there are a number of economic contentions.

First, let's talk money. We may have teased TV station executives earlier about their seemingly stingy tendencies, but they do have the right idea. Success in the video business is not achieved by wasting money on the flashiest new toys on the market—it's achieved by investing in quality tools that will help you do your job better. HDV is a smart investment. Current models of professional HDV camcorders start at around $3,000, and even the most expensive units are well under $10,000. Consumer HDV camcorders are even less, though they lack many of the professional features you will want or need on the job. Granted, a professional HDV camcorder may cost you a little more than some DV camcorders, but you are investing in HD. However, if you are going to spend comparable money on an SD camcorder, why would you not choose HD?

Part of your ongoing investment will be recording media. While many video professionals dream of a day when videotape has been replaced entirely by tapeless technologies, that day is not yet here. In the interim, the cost of recording media is an important consideration, and few options can compete with HDV. It uses MiniDV videotape, which costs about $4 for a consumer-grade, 60-minute cassette. Granted, you probably should not settle for the lowest quality (if you do, maybe you need to rethink the whole HD investment), so Sony's DVM-80PR premium MiniDV tape costs about $9. On the high end, JVC and Sony have introduced cassettes specifically for HDV, which promise significantly fewer errors and drop-outs. The JVC M-DV63ProHD costs about $14 per tape, while the Sony DigitalMaster PHDVM-63DM (shown in **Figure 2.2**) costs about $16 per tape. (JVC and Sony are not the only providers of high-end MiniDV tape; Maxell®, for example, offers DVPRO Master.)

Figure 2.2 Even top-of-the-line videotapes developed specifically for HDV, such as the Sony DigitalMaster, are economically priced compared to other HD formats. (Photo Courtesy of Sony)

In comparison, a 64-minute Sony HDCAM® tape in a large cassette costs close to $60, while a 64-minute Panasonic DVCPRO HD tape in a large cassette is around $32. A 32-minute small Sony HDCAM cassette costs about $30, while a 33-minute medium Panasonic DVCPRO cassette costs about $9. When it comes to tape, HDV is easily the lowest priced HD option. HDV even compares favorably to the analog workhorse, Betacam SP. A 60-minute Sony Betacam SP tape in a large cassette costs $18, while a 30-min-ute tape in a small cassette costs close to $10—and neither records HD.

Another benefit to HDV is flexibility. Every professional HDV camcorder on the market can record DV footage as well. (Some, like the Sony Z1, also record DVCAM.) This means you can choose to acquire footage in high definition or standard definition, depending on the needs of your project.

Your SD material will also benefit from the improved image processing that is inherent in HDV camcorders. There's an old saying in video production: garbage in, garbage out. It means that if you start with poor image quality, you are stuck with poor image quality. Oh, you might be able to make minimal improvements to the picture, but it won't be enough to hide the limitations of the original footage. The moral is to begin with the best possible images so you can deliver the best possible images.

As you remember from Chapter 1, when you acquire footage in HD, you record more picture information than when you record in SD. As a result, when you downconvert HD footage to SD, you are starting with more picture information, so your image will look better than if you recorded in SD in the first place. This process is called *oversampling* and it's another benefit to investing in HDV, even if you still primarily deliver SD projects.

Next, consider the return on your investment. Can you charge more for your services in HD? Kirk Barber, author of *The Wedding Video Handbook*, wrote in 2005 that his clients were not yet asking for HD quality videos; however, he believed it could change within a few years. What is the life cycle of your equipment? How long do you keep your camcorders? Is it worth investing in HDV today for potential business tomorrow? Is the improved picture quality of your SD material reason enough to make the investment?

The HDV Disclaimer

To be fair, HDV is not a perfect solution for all situations, nor has HDV received universal support by the video industry. For example, Panasonic officials have steadfastly maintained dissatisfaction with the HDV signal. As a result, the company has not introduced any HDV equipment, and instead has produced a competing low-cost HD camcorder using its own format. As you will learn in Chapter 3, HDV also brings its fair share of editing complications.

Plus, HDV is perceived by the industry as a low-end HD solution, which puts into question whether manufacturers will ever develop more robust camcorders based around the format. For example, officials at the BBC, which began broadcasting over-the-air HD in the United Kingdom in May 2006, see HDV as more of a DV replacement than a format with which to produce high-end dramatic HD content. That said, while it may not be a panacea for all entry-level HD ills, HDV is now a mature, established format with a variety of production and post-production equipment choices. For thousands of video professionals, it is "good enough" to make HD acquisition a reality.

Points of Interest

- As HDTVs become more common, SD programming will become less desirable for viewers.

- HDV is already being used by a variety of video professionals, from high-profile projects to one-man production crews.

- With its low-cost equipment and media, HDV is an economical HD production choice.

CHAPTER 3

Defining HDV

While the first two chapters of this book focused more on historical perspective and HDV applications, it's time to get technical. When you talk about digital video, there are a number of terms you simply cannot ignore. Product literature is loaded with descriptions and ratios that are about as coherent as a foreign language if you are not familiar with the concepts behind them. By the end of this chapter, however, you will have the information you need to understand the HDV specification chart that defines the format. Hopefully, this condensed course in digital video engineering will be relatively painless. Let's start small.

A Bit on Bits

When we talk about digital, we're talking about a binary language. At its most basic level, a digital system only knows *on*, which is represented by ones, or *off*, which is represented by zeros. In other words, either the signal exists or it does not exist.

Two important terms for our digital discussion are *bits* and *bytes*. A bit is a binary digit, a single one or zero, and it's the smallest unit of data in a digital system. Think of it as a sort of on/off switch, where one is on and zero is off. A group of bits that are processed together is called a byte. Basically, bits are the building blocks for bytes, which is not an easy thing to say but it's a central part of understanding digital video technology.

When you read camcorder technical specifications, you will see descriptions like "10-bit digital processing." What does that mean? Well, in that particular product, 10 bits make up a byte. The more bits in a byte, the more distinct the values in that byte. A 10-bit system has 1,024 discrete values; in other words, it has 10 on/off switches, and there are 1,024 different combinations of switches being on or off. It's easy to calculate how many discrete values are in a system. Simply take the number two (remember, it's a binary system) raised to the power of the number of bits. So, in the case of a 10-bit system, 2^{10} is 1,024.

An 8-bit system is a typical size, and it has 256 discrete values, 0 to 255 (you have to include the 0). That's a lot less than the 10-bit system we discussed. Again, it's a matter of simple mathematics: Each additional bit in your byte doubles the number of discrete values of on/off switch combinations.

One of the best ways to visualize the importance of bits and bytes is a grayscale. (See **Figures 3.1A, 3.1B,** and **3.1C.**) In a 1-bit grayscale, you only have two values, 0 and 1, where 0 is all off (black) and 1 is all on (white). Not much of a choice there. A 2-bit grayscale only gives you four values, 0 (0 percent white), 1 (33 percent white), 2 (67 percent white), and 3 (100 percent white). There's still not many shades of gray, but it's twice what you had in a 1-bit system. Compare that to the grayscale of an 8-bit system and you can see that more bits means more discrete values, which means a more accurate representation of the grayscale. (Technically, in the United States, black is not at value 0 and white is not at value 255 in digital video due to NTSC standards. For 8-bit systems, reference black is at 16 and reference white is at 235 to provide a buffer for broadcast.)

Figure 3.1A With a 1-bit grayscale, you have only two values—off (black) and on (white).

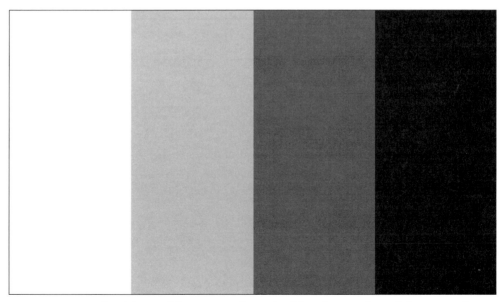

Figure 3.1B Each additional bit in your byte doubles the number of discrete values, so this 2-bit grayscale has twice as many combinations as the 1-bit grayscale.

Figure 3.1C An 8-bit grayscale is much more precise than the 1-bit or 2-bit grayscales.

How many bits do you need? Luckily, human eyes can be fooled pretty easily. An 8-bit system is more than acceptable to most people, and 10-bit video looks great even to most critical observers. Audio, however, is another story. Our ears are much more sensitive—we need at least 16-bit systems, though some experts argue that 20-bit or even 24-bit technology should be used to meet the needs of human hearing.

With all this talk about bits and bytes, it's important to understand that the images and sounds that you record digitally are actually analog in nature. Digital video is a representation of an analog signal. While there are numerous advantages to working with digital, it's nothing more than an approximation of the analog original. Even the information recorded in your digital camcorder is first captured in its original analog form, then converted into a digital signal.

So, how good is the digital copy of your analog information? That depends on how many times your analog-to-digital converter looks at the original, which is a process known as *sampling*. For broadcast audio, 48 kHz (48,000 times per second) is a typical *sampling frequency*. Compact discs, in comparison, have a 44.1-kHz sampling rate. For video, 13.5 MHz (13.5 million times per second) is also a common standard.

The quality of your digital copy also depends on the number of bits per sample you have, or the *quantization* of your digital data. Again, more is better; a 10-bit signal will have four times as many bits per sample as an 8-bit signal, so it will have higher accuracy.

Points of Interest

- Digital is an approximation of the original analog signal.

- The more bits in a byte, the more distinct the values in that byte.

- Audio and video quality are determined by sampling rate and the number of bits per sample.

Compression Basics

While you may not know much about digital video *compression* specifical-ly, there are examples of compression all around us. For example, concen-trated orange juice is compressed. The water is removed to make it more convenient to store and transport, and then you replace the water when you want to drink it. Compression is also common on the Internet; many people type "LOL" instead of "laughing out loud." It's a lot fewer char-acters, but it still conveys the idea that something is funny. Even a vanity license plate, such as "I LV ICE CRM," uses compression. Due to space limitations, the message has to leave out a few letters, but your brain fills in the missing information.

The essence of compression is throwing something away—and thinking you can replace it (or at least not miss it) later. Native uncompressed digi-tal video, and HD in particular, has an extremely high *bit rate*, or amount of information moving through the system each second, and requires large amounts of storage. For most applications, uncompressed digital video is simply impractical. Like our concentrated orange juice, we need to compress digital video for easy storage and transport. Digital video compression reduces both the bit rate and, therefore, the amount of data being stored.

Of course, there are concessions with compression. Concentrated orange juice might not taste as good as fresh squeezed, but it's usually good enough (and some people can't even taste the difference). With digital video, the compression tradeoff is a loss of picture quality, though some compression is so well engineered that most people can't even see or don't even notice the difference.

Compression discards information that is considered nonessential, can be easily reconstructed, or simply won't be perceived as missing by human eyes and ears. Using mathematical algorithms and predictions, compression reduces data by eliminating redundant information, and there's a lot of redundancy in digital video images.

Generally, compression systems fall into two categories, *lossless* and *lossy*.

As you might guess from the name, a lossless compression scheme completely restores all original data from the original image. As a result, the compression ratios are usually low and, as a result, do not reduce the bit rate sufficiently to be particularly effective for video.

Instead, most digital video uses a lossy video compression system. Lossy is more of an approximation rather than an exact duplicate of the data. As a result, a lossy system features higher compression ratios than a lossless system, so it is more efficient at dealing with the large amounts of data in digital video.

Basically, when an image is processed, the lossy compression scheme creates two groups of data. One group contains what is determined to be important information, which is kept. The other group is a collection of unimportant information, which is discarded. Unlike lossless, however, lossy is nonreversible. Once that information is gone, it's gone for good.

As previously mentioned, there's a lot of redundancy in video, which is one of the reasons why compression works. After all, if every frame of video was nothing but random pixels, there would be no way to determine which data to discard. Compression is possible because adjoining frames of video are more likely to be similar than different.

While lossy compression is probably a bad choice for your accounting software, it works just fine for digital video. Lossy compression algorithms take into account the fact that the human eye notices some picture elements more than others. For example, we are more sensitive to changes in the luminance, or brightness, of a video signal than in its chrominance, or color detail (such as hue and saturation). We are also more aware of moving objects than still objects. As a result, a lossy compression system can throw away more color information than brightness information. In fact, in most systems, color difference signals are sampled less frequently than luminance signals.

The digital video industry has a kind of shorthand using number ratios to describe sampling rate. There are three ratios that you will see frequently: *4:2:2*, *4:1:1*, and *4:2:0*. The first number represents the sampling rate of the luminance signal, while the second and third represent red and blue color differences. Easy enough, right? Unfortunately, there's a bit of an inconsistency in the shorthand that gets confusing.

As shown in **Figure 3.2**, "4" represents the sampling frequency, but the next numbers are actually fractions of that sampling frequency. As a result, in a 4:2:2 signal, the first "2," which represents the sampling rate of red color difference, would be 2/4, or 1/2, of the sampling frequency of the luminance. The same holds true for the blue color differences. In a 4:1:1 ratio, the red and blue color difference signals are sampled 1/4 as much as the luminance.

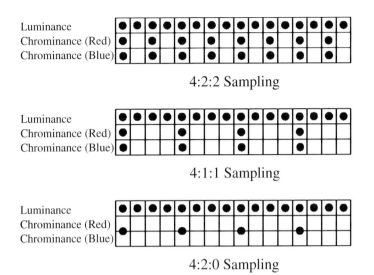

Figure 3.2 Sampling rates vary between 4:2:2, 4:1:1, and 4:2:0 systems.

The inconsistency lies in the 4:2:0 ratio. This does not mean that the blue color difference signals are not sampled. Instead, it means there are two color difference samples for every four luminance samples, one red and one blue, which are averaged from two adjacent lines in the field. Again, remembering that our eyes are less sensitive to color than brightness, even a 4:2:0 sampling rate can provide acceptable picture quality. That said, there are some systems that feature 4:4:4 sampling, where luminance, red color difference, and blue color difference are all sampled equally.

Points of Interest

- Compression keeps the amount of digital video data manageable by removing redundant or noncritical data.

- Most digital video uses lossy compression systems, which are more efficient than lossless systems because they discard data that is considered unimportant.

- Ratios like 4:2:2 represent the various sampling rates of luminance and color differences.

HDV Compression

Now that you have a basic understanding of how a digital signal is created and how it's compressed, let's apply those concepts to the HDV format specification. As you know, one of the main selling points of HDV is the idea of recording HD material on MiniDV videotape.

It's a familiar and relatively inexpensive form of media used by the video industry. Of course, to squeeze HD images on a tape originally designed for SD takes compression . . . a lot of compression.

MPEG-2 is the compression system used for HDV. It's a very popular compression system in the video industry, and it's available in a variety of "flavors." Not every application uses the highest quality video or requires the same amount of compression, so MPEG-2 was designed to be flexible. There are a number of Profiles and Levels to accommodate different needs. As shown in **Table 3.1**, there are four Levels of video quality, from low (consumer level) to high (high definition). There are also six Profiles, each with different sets of compression tools. So far, 12 compliance points within the grid have been defined.

Table 3.1 MPEG-2 Profiles and Levels. HDV uses MPEG-2 Main Profile at High-1440 Level.

	SIMPLE	MAIN		SNR SCALABLE	SPATIAL SCALABLE	HIGH
HIGH		4:2:0 1920 × 1152 80 Mbps I, P, B				4:2:0, 4:2:2 1920 × 1152 100 Mbps I, P, B
HIGH-1440		4:2:0 1440 × 1152 60 Mbps I, P, B			4:2:0 1440 × 1152 60 Mbps I, P, B	4:2:0, 4:2:2 1440 × 1152 80 Mbps I, P, B
MAIN	4:2:0 720 × 576 15 Mbps I, P	4:2:0 720 × 576 15 Mbps I, P, B	4:2:2 720 × 608 15 Mbps I, P, B	4:2:0 720 × 576 15 Mbps I, P, B		4:2:0, 4:2:2 720 × 576 20 Mbps I, P, B
LOW		4:2:0 352 × 288 4 Mbps I, P, B	4:2:2	4:2:0 352 × 288 4 Mbps I, P, B		

PROFILES

HDV uses MPEG-2 Main Profile at High-1440 Level. If you look at the description, you'll notice the now familiar 4:2:0 video sampling, as well as some other information. The 1440 × 1152 figure represents the number of pixels supported at High-1440 Level. Remember, HDV supports both 720p and 1080i video signals—and the number of pixels used in the HDV format standard varies based on the mode in which you are shooting. An HDV 720p signal has 1280 × 720 pixels, while a 1080i signal has 1440 × 1080 pixels. Notice that High Level in the chart supports far more pixels than necessary for HDV, while Main and Low Levels don't have sufficient resolution.

Also, MPEG-2 Main Profile at High-1440 Level supports up to 60 Mbps video bit rate, which is far more than HDV requires at either 720p (19 Mbps) or 1080i (25 Mbps). Again, however, Main and Low Levels have insufficient bit rate capabilities, and High Level is simply excessive. Finally, the I, P, and B represent special kinds of video frames that are crucial to the compression process, which will be discussed later.

MPEG-2 compression collects several video frames in sequence and forms a group of pictures, also known as a *GOP*. The redundant nature of successive video frames as shown in **Figure 3.3** is what makes this kind of compression possible—the system works to predict the differences between frames (motion estimation) while exploiting the similarities. The frames in a GOP work together to form a complete sequence of video images using as few bits as possible to accomplish the task. This technique is called interframe compression.

Figure 3.3 Why keep recreating the same blue sky? A shot like this that's held for even a second or two has a lot of repetitive information between frames. Interframe compression saves bits by predicting the differences between successive frames, rather than completely rebuilding each frame independently.

There are three different kinds of frames that can be present in a GOP. The frame with the most bits is the "I" frame, or intracoded frame. It is a self-contained frame of video, complete with its own *intraframe* compression. This type of compression is based on encoding the visual differences between pixels. It's the same compression technology used for DV. But HDV has a high definition signal with much more information than a DV signal, so more compression is required.

The I frame is basically the main frame of reference for other frames in the GOP, and there is only one I frame per GOP. A predicted frame, or "P" frame, uses information from previous I or P frames to construct its image. It has fewer bits than an I frame, as it only contains information that has changed. Then there is the bidirectional predictive frame, or "B" frame, which has the fewest bits of all. As the name implies, a B frame looks at preceding and following I or P frames to see what is different (MPEG-2 frames are encoded out of order).

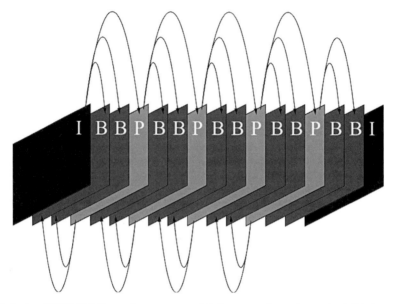

Figure 3.4 An HDV GOP can have up to 15 frames, though each GOP has only one I frame. Note the forward and backward predictive nature of the compression.

As shown in **Figure 3.4** a GOP can consist of a single I frame, or an I frame that's followed by a number of P frames, or an I frame that's followed by a combination of B and P frames. The next I frame starts a new GOP. There are only so many frames that can be included in a GOP before prediction errors (no one said the compression system was perfect) are no longer visually tolerable.

MPEG Influence

The Motion Picture Experts Group, or MPEG, is a working group of the International Organization for Standardization (ISO) and the International Electrotechnical Commission (IEC) that first met in 1988 to develop international standards for audio and video compression. While its MPEG-2 compression system is used extensively in the video industry (HDV, DVDs, DTV transmission, and more), the group has produced a number of other standards.

Approved in 1992, MPEG-1 was the group's first success story. Designed to encode audio and video up to about 1.5 Mbps, it is a far simpler compression scheme than later MPEG standards. MPEG-1 isn't broadcast-quality compression. However, in the years before DVDs were commonplace in personal computers, MPEG-1 was the compression technology that made it possible to play videos from CDs.

MPEG-4 builds on the success of MPEG-1 and MPEG-2. It allows the encoding of individual objects or audio elements, providing more flexibility and improved compression efficiency. There are also noncompression projects such as MPEG-7, officially known as the "Multimedia Content Description Interface," a collection of tools designed to describe multimedia content for efficient searching or browsing through content.

And part of the MPEG-1 compression system has literally changed the music industry. MPEG-1 Audio Layer III has become a very popular way to compress audio files for download over the Internet (both legally and illegally). Of course, most people simply refer to one of these music files as an MP3.

While MPEG-2 compression allows high definition recording at a relatively low bit rate, it is not exactly edit-friendly. What happens if you want your edit point on a P frame or B frame? Neither has all the visual information you need. MPEG-2 was not really designed for editing; it is more of a transport or distribution compression system that's been repurposed for HDV. The same interframe coding that makes HDV acquisition so efficient is what makes editing so problematic.

As you'll read in more detail in Chapter 6, manufacturers have devised a number of solutions to the HDV editing dilemma. There are a handful of nonlinear editing systems that can support native HDV editing. Native HDV editing means no generation loss when you capture the footage. However, some native MPEG-2 editing solutions are limited to I-frame cuts. Plus, native HDV editing is an incredible drain on your system's processing power. Need to play or edit your file? First, you need to decode the transport stream, and that means decoding an entire GOP because the frames are dependent on each other for information—talk about extra effort for your CPU. More about your editing options will be discussed in Chapter 6.

One of the most popular workarounds is to *transcode* (or convert) HDV transport stream into a format that is more amenable to editing, such as an AVI or QuickTime® file, which uses only intraframe compression. When the project is complete, you then transcode back to HDV for your master. One drawback to this solution, however, is that non-native HDV files tend to be much larger in size than the original, as frames are encoded individually instead of in GOPs.

Points of Interest

- MPEG-2 is the compression system used for HDV.

- HDV uses both intraframe and interframe compression techniques.

- While there are some native HDV editing choices, many systems choose to transcode HDV footage for easier editing.

HDV Specifications

HDV is a unique video format. It may follow the same rules as other digital video formats and use similar compression systems, but it has a distinct set of technical requirements. Now, with your knowledge of digital video and compression in general, and the HDV format in particular, the HDV specification chart shown in **Table 3.2** is much easier to understand.

Table 3.2 The HDV specification chart includes technical requirements for video, audio, and transport.

HDV Specifications

Media	MiniDV Cassette Tape	
Video Signal	720p/25/30/50/60	1080i/50/60
Number of Pixels	1280 × 720	1440 × 1080
Aspect Ratio	16:9	
Video Compression	MPEG-2 Main Profile at High-1440 Level	
Sampling Frequency for Luminance	74.25 MHz	55.7 MHz
Video Sampling Format	4:2:0	
Video Quantization	8 bit	
Video Bit Rate After Compression	19 Mbps	25 Mbps
Audio Compression	MPEG-1 Audio Layer II	
Audio Sampling Frequency	48 kHz	
Audio Quantization	16 bits	
Audio Bit Rate After Compression	384 kbps	
Audio Mode	Stereo (2 channels)	
Data Format	MPEG-2 System	
Stream Type	Transport Stream	Packetized Elementary Stream
Stream Interface	IEEE-1394 (MPEG-2 TS)	

As you know, HDV was designed to be recorded on MiniDV tape. While some manufacturers have already figured out how to record HDV on hard disk, optical disc, and other media, the original specification calls for the same videotape used in numerous DV camcorders already in service. HDV supports both 720p and 1080i acquisition in a number of frame rates, though both video signals are recorded in 16:9.

HDV's MPEG-2 "flavor" of choice (or compliance point) is Main Profile at High-1440 Level, which provides sufficient pixels and bit rate, as well as I, P, and B frame structure. Luminance is sampled at different frequencies, depending on whether 720p or 1080i have been selected, but either format offers 4:2:0 sampling and 8-bit quantization, taking advantage of our easily fooled eyes. After compression, 720p has a bit rate of 19 Mbps and 1080i has a bit rate of 25 Mbps, the same bit rate as DV. Audio specifications are also easier to understand. HDV uses an earlier MPEG audio compression system for its two-channel stereo sound, and has a sampling frequency of 48 kHz, 16-bit audio quantization, and 384-Mbps bit rate to compensate for our sensitive ears.

At the bottom of the chart are specifications for data and transport. The data format is the MPEG-2 system, due to HDV's use of MPEG-2 compression. Stream type is simply the method by which audio and video data are combined for the MPEG-2 system. Remember, with its GOP-based compression, you have to think of native HDV as more of a data transport stream than individual frames of video. With its lower bit rate, 720p utilizes a transport stream, while a packetized elementary stream is used for 1080i. Finally, stream interface refers to the data transmission standard. The HDV MPEG-2 transport stream is transmitted over IEEE-1394 (or FireWire®), which has become an almost ubiquitous standard in NLE systems.

These first three chapters have provided you with a solid foundation for working with HDV. You have historical perspective on HDTV and how it is impacting the U.S. consumer marketplace, as well as some business insight and a basic technical understanding of the HDV format and its specifications. Now it's time to apply that knowledge to the HDV production process. Chapter 4 begins the process with a look at the current crop of HDV production equipment, including cameras, accessories, and VTRs.

Points of Interest

- HDV is a high definition, widescreen format that supports interlaced and progressive video signals at a variety of frame rates.

- MPEG-2 compression creates a bit rate low enough so HDV can be recorded on MiniDV videotape.

- HDV is transmitted over IEEE-1394, a popular interface for today's video workflow.

CHAPTER 4

HDV Camcorders

Since the first HDV camcorder was introduced in 2003, there have been a number of consumer HDV camcorders, often versions of the professional models with fewer features, which we will discuss briefly. We will focus mainly on professional HDV products.

Before really getting into how HDV camcorders function, it is important to understand the principles behind the image acquisition—in other words, the chips. Chips have replaced the older tubes that converted light into electrical impulses.

Chip Comparisons

Today's camcorders use one of two different chip technologies: the *Charge Coupled Device* (CCD) or the *Complementary Metal Oxide Semiconductor* (CMOS). CCDs have been around for decades, while CMOS chips have only been used in a handful of video cameras since the late 1990s. However, CMOS technology has been well established in the digital still-photography market.

Without going into detail on how a CCD works, it is better to understand how the CMOS differs. Antiquated tube technology was replaced with the CCD chip, and the CMOS chip technology offers improvements over CCDs. CMOS has its own class of integrated circuits. Within these "circuits" resides a microcontroller, microprocessor, random access memory (RAM), and several other digital logic circuits. The circuit only uses power when its internal transistors are switching on and off between states. It is considered an improvement over CCD technology because it produces less heat, uses less power, costs less to produce, and actually conducts more logic functions on the chip.

By the way, the "metal" of CMOS was aluminum, but it is no longer used in the manufacture of a CMOS chip—it has been replaced with polysilicon. The name has remained the same even though silicon is used instead of metal. (This same term, CMOS, is sometimes used to refer to the non-volatile memory in a computer, so don't let that confuse you.)

Developed in 1963 at Fairchild Semiconductor by Frank Wanlass, the first integrated circuits using CMOS technology were not incorporated until RCA® did it in 1968. Produced in an effort to save battery life, CMOS was still years away from being used in video cameras. By the early 1990s, digital integrated circuits were using CMOS technology. Because of the need for downsizing in these circuits, the CMOS chip's higher energy efficiency, faster operating speed, smaller size, and cheaper production costs made it a natural choice. The same qualities could not be found with other transistors.

All was not perfect with the earlier CMOS circuits—electrostatic discharge could easily damage these fragile circuits. Better protection circuitry had to be developed, but static is still a problem with any computer circuit.

The CCD represented a major improvement over the pickup tube in earlier video cameras. Tube cameras had several limitations. They could not be pointed at bright objects or the image would "burn in" to the tube. In addition, the camera could not be pointed down or particles could collect on the front of the tube, and the tubes had to be constantly aligned or "registered" because they would drift out of adjustment. The CCD corrected all of those problems.

The CMOS chip has come even farther by improving on the low light issues and power consumption of the CCD. Consumers want cameras that can record their child's birthday party in candlelight without mountains of grain. They are not concerned about the technology that makes it possible—they just want that capability. Plus, the cost savings of manufacturing CMOS chips is an added benefit.

Consumer Quality

If the current crop of professional HDV camcorders is too expensive for your budget, a handful of consumer-level HDV camcorders are also on the market. Available at a lower cost than their professional counterparts, these camcorders often share a similar body style and optics, but are missing many of the features required (or at least highly desired) by professional videographers. For example, the Sony HDR-FX1 bears a striking resemblance to the Z1, but it does not have XLR audio inputs or phantom power for microphones.

Figure 4.1 The Sony HDR-HC3 camcorder. (Photo courtesy of Sony)

The FX1 is also missing a DVCAM record mode, auto focus assist, and time code.

When Sony introduced its A1 HDV camcorder in 2005, the HDR-HC1 Handycam consumer version was also announced. The following year, Sony upgraded the consumer unit to the HDR-HC3 Handycam camcorder, which was even more compact but still lacked time code, XLR inputs, and other professional features However, the price tag reflects the cut corners, as the consumer HC3 lists for about half the price of the A1 (see **Figure 4.1**).

The trend to offer consumer versions of professional HDV camcorders began in 2003, when JVC released the GR-HD1, a consumer version of the first HDV professional camcorder, the

JY-HD10U. Now, low-cost HD camcorders without professional equivalents are beginning to enter the consumer marketplace. For example, Sanyo introduced the Xacti HD1 in 2006. It weighs less than a pound, records on SD memory cards, and has a built-in flash for still images. While it is certainly lacking in professional features and records in MPEG-4 (so it's not HDV), the HD1 lists for less than $800.

JVC Strikes First

The JVC Corporation has been known for developing several firsts in the industry. When video was in its infancy, JVC developed a video tape cassette that could be used by the average consumer that would record up to six hours of material on one tape. That invention was called *VHS* (Vertical Helical Scan or Video Home System). As time progressed, the standard developed by Sony, *Betamax*, lost favor with customers and ended up evolving into a high-quality broadcast standard (*Betacam*), and JVC's VHS hung around.

The first HDV camcorder was developed by JVC. Although now discontinued, the JVC JY-HD10U, released in 2003, recorded 720p/30 footage on a 60-minute MiniDV videocassette (see **Figure 4.2**). HDV was born.

Figure 4.2 JVC's JY-HD10U camcorder. (Photo courtesy of JVC)

Professional and prosumer cameras of the early 21st century were all sporting three CCD chips because only consumers were using the less expensive, one-chip CCD camcorders. If you wanted high-quality "broadcast" video, you needed three chips. The factors that would determine the price and the image quality of a camcorder were twofold: the size and number of the chips. One-chip cameras used the same circuit for the red, green, and blue images, where a three-chip model would use a CCD for each color—allowing better separation.

Professional cameras used the largest 2/3-inch chips in their CCDs. (*Note:* Actually, 1-inch CCD chips could be found in studio cameras, but we will be discussing only portable cameras.) Most home camcorders would start with either one or three 1/6-inch chips. The next size up and improvement would be the 1/4-inch CCD. Camcorders stalled in this area for quite some time. Sony and Panasonic introduced the larger 1/3-inch chips and the pixel count increased. It makes sense that the larger the area of the chip, the more pixels could reside there. Larger camcorders over $6,000 were using 1/2-inch chips for extremely sharp images.

When every other prosumer camera on the block had three 1/4 or 1/3-inch chips, JVC introduced the first HDV camcorder utilizing one CCD chip—a 1,180,000-pixel chip. At the time, most others had CCDs with about 400,000 pixels per chip range. This progressive-scan chip would mask the single CCD chip to shoot images in high definition's 16:9 aspect ratio.

The HD10U would play back both 1080i/60 and 720p/60. It was interesting that the camera would play back footage shot in 1080i when all other cameras shooting in that format were not using MiniDV tape—a difficult feat to produce. The HD10U would also shoot standard definition at 480i/60 and enhanced definition at 480p/60. It sported a F1.8 lens specially designed for high definition (though it did not appear to differ from an SD lens). MPEG-4 footage could be recorded onto an SD memory card, and the camera even included new PC software that provided very basic MPEG-2 editing capability. All this could be had for a price of slightly less than $3,000.

The unique setup of this camera, according to *Newbie Products* reviewer Cammy Stevenson, was that it utilized "a unique hybrid complementary primary color filter array, capable of producing 1280 × 720p high-definition resolution." It had all of the other features a camcorder should have: a 3.5-inch color LCD monitor, color viewfinder, a 10× zoom lens, and an IEEE-1394 connection for importing footage into NLE systems. "You will be impressed how this high definition camcorder performs with par excellence with other competitors," Stevenson continued. "Overall, at this price range, nothing can match the features of this camera—a great offer for a great camcorder."

Of course, those using the vastly more expensive "real" HD cameras said that the JVC was not "genuine" HD, that it didn't compare with Varicam or HDCAM footage. And they were right—the footage did look good, a noticeable improvement over SD, but nowhere near the quality of "real" HD. In JVC's defense, the company had delivered a true HD camcorder at the price point of many SD camcorders. No video professional with even a tenuous grip on reality would expect a $3,000 camcorder to match the visual quality of a camera that used a lens that cost close to $20,000. Naysayers aside, JVC had opened the door to low-cost HD video production with its HDV camcorder.

Sony brought its own one-chip camcorder to market in the early 21st century with its HVR-A1U. This camcorder featured a more light-friendly CMOS chip. The 1/3-inch, 2,968,000-pixel chip was capable of recording in 1080i, DVCAM (Sony's DV format that records 40 minutes on a standard MiniDV cassette), and MiniDV. (See **Figure 4.3**.) Imagine, a chip

Figure 4.3 Sony's HVR-A1U camcorder features a CMOS imager. (Photo courtesy of Sony)

with almost three million pixels, more than twice of number of pixels in JVC's one-chip camcorder.

This little camera produced large results. Weighing in at less than two pounds, it certainly did not look like an HD camera. If used by soccer moms and dads to document the big game, it certainly would not stand out when compared to other camcorders. Students found it to be an affordable alternative to the three-CCD SD camcorders costing just as much—and they would be shooting in HDV!

Despite its size, it has all of the features of larger models, such as an LCD monitor, IEEE-1394 connectivity, XLR inputs—and something that the JVD did not offer with the HD10U . . . *downconversion* capabilities. Using the touch screen on the LCD monitor, you can select shooting in 1080i HDV, but you can also change that footage to SD and let the camera do the conversion. Currently, Sony is the only HDV manufacturer that allows on-board downconversion.

Before we discuss downconversion in detail, let's look at how the camera performs in the shooting arena. Using a single CMOS chip, the lens still does not allow all of the CMOS's pixels to be utilized. In reality, this is an SD camera that is able to shoot in HD. In the HDV mode, you are only using most and not all of the pixels—masking still occurs. When shooting in 16:9 and in 1080i, you still have more choices, even though you are shooting in 30 frames per second.

As we discussed in Chapter 2, 24p is a popular frame rate for shooting, as 24 frames per second in progressive-scan mode emulates the jittery look of film. The Sony A1 does not offer 24p, but it does have an interlaced version of it. In the menu, you can select "CineFrame® 24," which converts the 30 fps to 24 fps. The camera also offers "CineFrame 30," which shoots in 30 fps.

24p and 24i (for lack of a better term) do not look the same. The frame rates may be identical, but interlaced and progressive footage have a different look. Remember, interlaced frames are composed of two fields, while progressive frames are displayed in their entirety. While one complete frame of an interlaced image may look identical to one complete frame of a progressive image, the perceived movement during playback will be different.

If you viewed still frames of an image shot in 24 frames progressive and 24 frames interlaced, the images would be virtually identical. The human eye cannot detect scan lines. If we could slow the frames down and see how the image was assembled, there would be a sizeable difference. But when both progressive and interlaced formats are played, there is a visible difference. The *persistence of vision* effect in the brain converts these successive single frames to a blurred motion and we then perceive movement.

Sony also added a movie-like look to its CineFrame 24 mode by changing the gamma (color values). The image does have more of a movie theatre look. The colors are richer and the saturation is increased. The same effect may be seen on a video projector when you select a "cinema" setting. The blacks become deeper and richer. (Because the images in this book are not in color, we won't attempt to illustrate this point here.)

After all of the improvements in technology, we are still trying to create the film look in a video camera. Video's harshness is too real and crisp, and HD footage (including HDV) makes that fact even more evident. By slowing the frame rate and imitating film's jerky quality, the viewer perceives images that more closely resemble film.

Again, if you put two CineFrame 24 images side by side, one with the Cinema gamma increased, you would notice a slight color differentiation, but that would not be evident in a black-and-white photo (so it will not appear in this book).

Points of Interest

- CMOS technology, already a mainstay in digital still cameras, produces less heat and uses less power than the CCD chips that are used in the majority of today's video cameras.

- JVC introduced the first HDV camcorder, a one-CCD unit, in 2003.

- Some camcorders that only shoot in interlaced mode attempt to emulate the 24p film look by shooting 24 frames per second and adjusting gamma settings.

Change Your Image

As we mentioned earlier, the Sony A1 HDV camcorder offers in-camera downconversion. In Chapter 6 we will go into more detail with editing in HDV versus downconverting the footage to standard definition. But since the A1U does that for you, it is worth mentioning that here also. Once your HDV footage has been shot in 1080i, and in the 16:9 aspect ratio in either in the CineFrame 24 mode or at 30 fps you have the choice of editing that footage natively in the format you recorded it in, or changing or downconverting that to standard definition.

This may be a necessity depending on the end use of your material.

Sony offers the user four choices in this mode once the FireWire (IEEE-1394) cable—or as Sony refers to it, the *iLink*®—is connected from the camera to your editing system. Obviously, one choice is to send the footage to your system in the same format it was shot in; if that is the case, simply select "HDV" as your output choice on the menu. If instead you desire to downconvert your footage, your selection would be "downconvert." Here you are given three different options from which to choose in your downconversion to standard definition: *letterbox*, *squeeze*, or *edge crop*.

Letterbox

Letterbox, as the name implies, is when you have black bands at the top and bottom of the screen, similar to a mailbox letter slot (which was the inspiration for the name). This mode takes all of the visual picture information you shot in the 16:9 aspect ratio and makes it fit on a 4:3 aspect ratio screen. If the image is flattened with horizontal bars at the top and bottom of the screen, you can show the image at its original width, even though the image itself does not fill the entire height of the 4:3 screen. In fact, before the advent of HDV, editors who wanted their SD footage to look like it was shot in widescreen would add black bands to the top and bottom of the screen to simulate letterbox.

Here is where the terminology may become confusing. With letterbox, the image looks like a letterbox, with the horizontal bands at the top and bottom of the screen. With widescreen, the image fills the 16:9 screen without the black bands. See **Figures 4.4** and **4.5**.

Figure 4.4 An image displayed in letterbox.

Figure 4.5 An image displayed in widescreen.

When you rent or purchase a DVD, you are sometimes given the option of watching the film in widescreen, letterbox, or *fullscreen* (pan and scan). If you choose to watch the movie in widescreen, the full image will be displayed on your 16:9 aspect ratio television with no visible bands. If you have a 4:3 set, that same widescreen image will be squeezed, so actors will look rather tall and thin. All of the visual 16:9 information must fit on a 4:3 screen, resulting in a compressed image. The title frame of old movies, such as *Around the World in Eighty Days*, were sometimes displayed on TV screens like this in the 1960s and 1970s, so the name of the film would fit on the viewer's TV screen.

Showing vital information is what prompted *pan and scan* to be created, in which a computer scans each frame of a 16:9 (or wider) film and focuses on the important action. For example, if two people are talking, one at the left and one at the right side of the screen, the computer determines who is talking and pans over to that person. It's not a perfect system; the "camera" has to move slowly from one person to the other, so you always miss some vital footage. Plus, artistically, it is not the way the director envisioned the film to be viewed.

On the big screen of the theatre, the wide aspect ratio was not a problem. When films were sold to television, however, they had to be converted (panned and scanned) to fit on the smaller screen. Also, keep in mind that most TVs were generally much smaller than the larger screens of today. Letterbox, while not particularly problematic on a 50-inch TV, is much less appealing to most people on a 13-inch screen. **Figures 4.6**, **4.7**, and **4.8** illustrate how the original widescreen footage is changed to fit on a smaller aspect ratio screen.

Figure 4.6 The original widescreen image.

Figure 4.7 The image is panned to the left to reveal that person while they speak.

Figure 4.8 The image is then panned to the right to catch the other person talking in the 4:3 frame.

If you choose letterbox, the image is displayed as we mentioned earlier with the black bands appearing at the top and bottom of the screen. All of the footage is visible, the way the director envisioned it, but the image is smaller on the screen because of the letterbox effect.

Finally, if the 4:3 mode or fullframe is selected, pan and scan is still incorporated, but the entire screen is filled with the image, although some of the image has been cut off. Often, if fullframe is selected, a disclaimer appears on the screen that declares the film has been modified from its original aspect ratio to fit your screen. In the age of disclaimers, the producers just want you to know that you are not watching the film in the way it was originally intended to be viewed—consider yourself warned.

If letterbox is your choice in downconversion, be comforted in knowing that the entirety of your frame will be displayed on the 4:3 screen, along with the telltale black bars at the top or bottom. This is the most widely selected format because essentially nothing is lost in the transfer process. See **Figures 4.9** and **4.10**.

Figure 4.9 The original widescreen image.

Figure 4.10 The same widescreen image downconverted to letterbox preserves the entire frame, though the image is bracketed by black bars on the screen.

Squeeze

Another option when shooting in HDV is to squeeze your image so it fits on the 4:3 screen. This mode simply takes the 16:9 footage and compresses both sides so the same image fits on your 4:3 screen. Why would anyone want their images squeezed? Some people choose this method because they want the entire image on the screen but do not like the space the black letterbox bands take. Instead, they edit all of the footage on a 4:3 screen (squeezed), and then they expand the footage back to its original widescreen size for display on 16:9 sets.

This does take another step in the post process, but there are those purists who do not like letterbox and want the image displayed as a full 16:9 image. Also, many owners of 16:9 TV sets want the full area of the image to be displayed. If watching a 4:3 signal on a 16:9 screen, you see black bands on both sides of the image instead of the top and bottom. Some sets offer the option of expanding the image so it fills the screen—instead of slimming everyone, it makes them appear fatter—but at least the screen is filled. If squeeze is selected and the image is expanded in post, it will still fill the 16:9 screen. **Figures 4.11** and **4.12** illustrate the squeezing process.

Figure 4.11 A widescreen image in 16:9.

Figure 4.12 The same widescreen image downconverted and squeezed.

Edge Cropping

The last downconversion option is to edge crop. Essentially, it means the material on the left and right of the screen is cropped and removed. Much like when you are cropping out unneeded information on a still photograph, you are removing what was on the left and right sides of the frame.

Again, this option is for people who want to fill their 4:3 screens with an image and choose not to have letterbox bands. Vital information may be lost in this process if the editor selects the crop option without the director's approval. If the shot had been framed with the 4:3 aspect ratio in mind, edge cropping will lose no vital information. It's a common practice that keeps the important action in the "safe area" in the middle of the frame. Once this mode has been selected in the downconversion process, the edge-cropped footage is gone and cannot be retrieved in post (unless the original HDV source footage is used). This principle is shown in **Figures 4.13** and **4.14**.

Figure 4.13 The original widescreen image.

Figure 4.14 The same image that has been subjected to edge cropping.

> ### Points of Interest
>
> - Letterbox shows the entire 16:9 frame on a 4:3 set, but fills the rest of the screen with black bands.
>
> - A squeezed image maintains the entire 16:9 frame but squeezes it into a 4:3 monitor, so people and objects look taller and thinner.
>
> - As the name implies, edge crop (or fullscreen) cuts off the sides of a 16:9 image so it can fit on a 4:3 screen.

Three-Chip Camcorders

The Sony A1 has a few tricks that the JVC's HD10U did not: It can shoot in 1080i (the HD10U could only playback 1080i), downconvert in the camera, and has twice the pixel count. This is another advantage of the CMOS chip—it allows more light into the camera (less grainy footage by not increasing the gain), so more pixels can be crammed into less space (one chip doing the work of three).

Currently, there are no low-end camcorders with three CMOS chips, but that could change in the near future. To date, the A1 is the highest quality, single-chip camcorder on the market (not including high-end digital cinema cameras from companies like ARRI and Dalsa). This, too, will change as other manufacturers create entry-level camcorders. Meanwhile, a handful of manufacturers have introduced three-CCD HDV camcorders.

JVC GY-HD100U

JVC's first entry into the three-CCD arena is the GY-HD100U. This is another trendsetter for JVC, because it was the first HDV camera to offer interchangeable lenses. A Fujinon® 5.5mm-to-88mm lens is standard and allows shooting down to seven Lux. See **Figure 4.15**. Using three CCDs with 1.6 million pixels each, this camera was also the first HDV offering that used the full raster of the CCD, rather than just a standard definition camera converted to an HDV model.

Figure 4.15 The JVC HY-HD100U was the first HDV camcorder that allowed interchangeable lenses. (Photo courtesy of JVC)

One of the HD100U's strengths is its multiple recording modes: 720p/60/30/24, as well as 720p/50/35 for Europe. The camcorder also offers SD recording options: 24p and 30i.

If you shoot in HDV, your footage cannot be downconverted, and the FireWire output needs to be set to HDV (not DV). (JVC thought that the extra cost and weight of the circuitry needed for downconversion was not needed.) That does not mean that the JVC only exports native HDV. Here, too, you have options: You can output 720p, 1080i (even though the camera does not record 1080i), 480p, or SD. The tape playback can be selected to use the RCA component or composite output rather than FireWire to playback in the following formats: DV, in which the footage is output in squeezed format only with no letterbox or edge crop options; HDV, which outputs high definition footage through the RCA connectors; DVCAM, Sony's higher speed format; or auto, which automatically decides for you. The same output RCA terminal on the camera can be menu selected to output component or composite.

The Focus Assist is a standard feature with the HD100U that converts your viewfinder or LCD screen image to blue. This allows more ease in focusing the image if the normal colors are removed and everything is fringed with blue. There is really nothing not to like about the HD100U—it's inexpensive, it can be optioned to the hilt, and it records some impressive images.

In mid-2006, JVC upgraded its GY-HD100U by introducing the GY-HD110U, which has the same physical appearance of the earlier model. In fact, almost all features and performance specifications are the same. There are, however, a number of improvements. The HD110U offers a black and white mode for the viewfinder, adjustable settings for focus assist, and a choice of letterbox, squeeze, or edge crop for composite out. On the audio side, the HD110U provides 13-segment audio level indicator, manual audio control while in full auto shooting mode, and an audio limiter in manual mode.

Sony HVR-Z1U

Sony's first professional three-CCD camcorder market offering is the HVR-Z1U (see **Figure 4.16**). It shares most of the same specifications with the HDR-FX1, a camcorder aimed at the consumer market. However, the Z1 has XLR inputs. Audio inputs alone do not make a camera professional, but low-impedance inputs are certainly the right way to go with HDV.

Figure 4.16 Sony's HVR-Z1U HDV camcorder. (Photo courtesy of Sony)

Beginning its life as a DSR-PD150, maturing into the PD170, and finally blossoming as the Z1, Sony's HDV flagship boasts DVCAM and HDV recording capabilities. In HDV, the Z1 records in 1080i/50/60/30/25/24. (The 50 and 25 are Europe's standards for PAL HD.) Using "native" 16:9, 1/3-inch CCDs, the full area of the chips can be used for shooting. The black camera fits easily in your hands or on a lightweight tripod. And, as mentioned earlier in this chapter, the downconversion feature of Sony's cameras is extremely helpful.

The Z1U has a unique feature called *Color Correction*. In this mode the user can adjust the color of a specific object without changing the color of other items in the shot. Much like the *Selective Colorization* effect used in the movie *Pleasantville*, you could have someone wearing a green sweater and everything else in the shot could be black and white. This saves a lot of time in post and in Adobe After Effects®. Up to two distinct colors can be selected and the color phase of each adjusted in terms of gain.

Another feature unique to the Sony is that the color viewfinder can be switched to black and white for ease of focus. The flip-out 16:9 LCD monitor always remains in living color. Instead of fringing everything in blue, Sony chose to use black and white because focusing is easier without the distraction of color. In addition, you can use the viewfinder and the LCD screen at the same time.

Sony's *Hypergain*® feature allows shooting in low light conditions of less than three Lux by raising the gain above the normal 18 dB cutoff (with very little added grain). *4:3 Marker* and *Safety Zone* are features that display the 4:3 zones (useful if downconverting) and where the safe area resides in 4:3 or 16:9.

The *CineFrame Mode*, also mentioned earlier, gives the user the ability to shoot in "cinema like" mode in 30, 25, or 24 fps. The *Cinematone*® feature allows selectable gamma adjustment if shooting in 60 or 50 fps.

Using "native" 16:9 1/3-inch Super HAD™ CCDs, the full area of the chips can be used for shooting. The black camera fits easily in your hands or on a lightweight tripod. Essentially the same size as the PD170, the Z1U is simple to operate and no one knows you are shooting in HDV until they get close enough to notice the vibrant blue HDV illuminated on the side of the camera.

Canon XL H1

Canon has been wildly successful with its professional SD camcorders, the XL1, XL1s, and XL2. The new step up to HDV, introduced in 2005, is the XL H1 (see **Figure 4.17**), a jet-black camera that retains the great features of previous models and adds HDV functionality. It's the most expensive of the first batch of HDV camcorders, but it does offer some unique features.

Figure 4.17 The Canon XL H1 HDV camcorder. (Photo courtesy of Canon)

Canon also uses three 1/3-inch CCDs, but upped the pixel count from 600,000 to 1,670,000 pixels—the most pixels per chip available at the time in HDV. Like the Sony, these CCD sensors are native 16:9. Even the glass up front is a full 20× zoom lens from 5.4mm (1/10mm less than JVC's 5.5mm lens on the HD100U) to 108mm (20mm more than the JVC). The Canon XL H1 offers 1080i/60/30/24 shooting.

One feature noticeably absent from the XL H1 is an LCD panel. Instead, the camcorder sports a 2.4-inch, 16:9 color viewfinder, with an eyepiece that flips up to expose the LCD screen (in case more than one person needs to take a look). The JackPack on the back of the camera is a professional feature that can be used to clip the receiver of a wireless microphone or a larger, longer-lasting, brick battery pack. The professional BNC connectors (rather than prosumer RCA) even offer a "genlock," which is never seen on cameras at this price point. The XL H1 is also the first HDV camcorder to have four-channel independent audio controls. Sometimes two extra, controllable tracks are needed when recording audio.

Of course, XLR connections are included as well as another first—at least to our eyes. Every input and output opening is covered by a flexible rubber cap (nothing new there) but it is labeled by what resides underneath the cap. You no longer have to blindly open everything up to find the FireWire port or some other connection. The rubber cap displays "FireWire," so you know exactly where to go.

Being the most expensive and heaviest of the initial run of HDV cameras, Canon wanted a more film-camera appearance. With the large, heavy lens up front, handholding the Canon gets tiresome after a few hours.

Canon also expanded its HDV lineup in late 2006 with the XH A1 (see **Figure 4.18**) and the XH G1, both priced lower than the XL H1. The new camcorders don't offer the option of interchangeable lenses, though they sport built-in 20× zoom lenses with image stabilization. Both feature three 1/3-inch CCDs and provide 1080i/24/30/60 recording. The XH G1 includes the *JackPack* connectivity of the XL H1 as well.

As of this writing, these are all of the professional HDV camcorders available.

Figure 4.18 Canon's XH A1 (pictured) and XH G1 camcorders offer lower cost HDV alternatives to the XL H1, but don't have interchangeable lenses. (Photo courtesy of Canon)

Shuffling the Decks

Although HDV camcorders can be used as transfer devices to incorporate your footage into a nonlinear editing system, a few HDV decks are also available. JVC offers the BR-HD50E HDV recorder, which looks like a smaller version of the older Betacam SP rack-mounted deck. It can play back all the formats JVC could (720p) and could not (1080i) shoot.

Sony offers the HVR-M10 HDV recorder (**Figure 4.19**), which contains a three-inch color LCD monitor on the faceplate, as well as the same downconversion capabilities as its camcorders. It will downconvert and play back footage shot in 1080i, DVCAM, and MiniDV, as well as 720p footage shot with a JVC camcorder. Using the same MiniDV tapes makes compatibility easy.

Figure 4.19 The Sony HVR-M10 HDV deck. (Photo courtesy of Sony)

A Look at Lenses

The basic production process for an HD lens is almost identical to that of an SD lens—the big difference is that specifications are more exacting because of the additional resolution involved. In other words, more resolution requires better optics. Lenses have evolved from the older, standard definition days of yore.

The least expensive of the pack was the fixed lens on the discontinued JVC JY-HD10U. As your only nonremovable option, the JVC lens was the same one they had used in their SD line—this time it was just mated with an HDV camera. The 10× zoom range was adequate and the images recorded were sharp enough, but lenses would improve with later HDV camcorders. Sony made a vast improvement with its Z1 lens, manufactured by Carl Zeiss, one of the premiere German lens makers. Optically superior to the HD10U, Sony even improved on the version included on the PD170.

With the HD100U, JVC was still offering an SD lens on an HDV camcorder, but it was removable and made by Fujinon, which had been a major force in high-end broadcast lenses for quite some time. The CCD chips were still "native" and the optics had to be sharp. Compared side by side with Sony's Zeiss lens, the same footage shot in 720p (on the JVC) and 1080i (on the Sony) were light years apart—the detail in areas like skin and the texture of clothing were far sharper on the JVC because of its lens, which is optically superior to the lens on the Z1.

The Canon XL-H1's 20× HD lens is the first lens made specifically for an HDV camcorder. It looks like the 20× lens on the XL2 (except its case is black instead of white) and features an *optical image stabilizer*, which helps eliminate some of the unsteadiness in handheld shots. Just as the JVC HD100U outperforms the Sony Z1 in optics, the Canon XL H1 wins out over the JVC. The optics are clearly sharper on the Canon. Keep in mind, however, that the XL H1 is the most expensive HDV camcorder of the three.

Don't Forget To Accessorize

Clothes might make the man, but accessories make the videographer. You need more than a camcorder for a successful shoot. Beyond audio and lighting requirements, camera accessories can help you get the look you want. Before you begin shooting HDV, be sure you have the proper support equipment in your kit.

Companies like Century Optics offer a variety of lens adapters for HDV camcorders, which is a godsend for camcorders like the Sony Z1 that don't have a removable lens. Lens adapters allow you to change the optical characteristics of your lens for more shot variety. For example, a teleconverter allows you to extend your zoom capabilities, a wide-angle adapter allows you to shoot a wider angle of view, and a fisheye adapter provides unique, exaggerated depth.

Most camcorders have built-in neutral density (ND) filters, which are designed to control depth of field of exposure. However, companies like Tiffen and Schneider Optics provide filters that can radically change and improve the look of your video. Polarizing filters, for example, control glare and reflections on windows, while diffusion filters can soften your image. There are also filters to correct for light temperature, affect contrast, or even enhance a particular color without affecting the other colors in your image. Generally, filters are housed in a matte box attached to the front of your lens.

Arguably one of the biggest frustrations for HDV camcorder users is battery power. Because of the small form factor of cameras like the Sony Z1, professional "brick" batteries are not really an option, so Anton/Bauer® introduced the Elipz™ product line in 2006 (see **Figure 4.20**).

Figure 4.20 The Anton/Bauer Elipz provides an under-the-camcorder solution for power, while the EgripZ is a camera support option.

The battery, mounted under the camera and positioned between the camcorder and its tripod, provides improved running times without the need for a battery belt. (Some of the larger HDV camcorders can be adapted to handle brick batteries.) Anton/Bauer also introduced ElightZ™, an on-camera light, and EgripZ™, a camera support grip, to complement its new battery solution.

Camera support is an important consideration for HDV camcorder shooters. While some models are designed for shoulder use (such as the Canon XL H1 or JVC HD100U), smaller camcorders lend themselves to more freestyle, handheld shooting. Unfortunately, the handheld look is not always desirable. Plus, while built-in optical stabilization is a helpful tool, it doesn't solve all your shaky problems. You definitely need to consider an investment in a tripod, as well as other camera support tools.

A tripod is standard operating equipment for a video professional. While HDV camcorders are lighter than professional camcorders of the past, you still need a solid, dependable tripod so you can get the steady shots for your various projects. A truly professional tripod, however, will probably not be found in a consumer electronics store. In other words, you've made a solid investment in your camera; make sure it is being supported by an equally solid tripod. Be sure your three-legged investment includes a fluid head, which will provide smooth pans and tilts.

A jib can bring even more versatility to your tripod. Basically, a jib is a counterbalanced "arm" that gives you extended reach with your camcorder. It can give you higher high-angle and lower low-angle shots than a standard tripod, plus it can be useful for more dramatic camera moves. Some models even provide focus and zoom control, so you can adjust your shot even when your camcorder is several feet above you. The downside of using a jib, however, is that even a smaller model is obtrusive. As a result, they can be rather limited in usefulness in small areas, far too distracting for some live events (such as weddings), and unwelcome when you are part of a crowd of videographers.

Smaller DV and HDV camcorders have also inspired a number of camera support systems. In the past few years, the marketplace has been flooded with products designed to assist handheld shots. Most redistribute the weight of the camcorder across your body so it is easy to hold your camcorder steady for longer periods of time. Others, like the Manfrotto Fig Rig (see **Figure 4.21**), do not attach to your body, but provide you with steadier shots on the move. These camera support systems can be very helpful (you'll need to practice), but some models can be surprisingly pricey.

Figure 4.21 The Fig Rig is one of many camera support systems designed to improve handheld shooting.

Finally, it is important to consider the transport of your gear. A professional camcorder is going to face enough abuse in the field, so you want to make sure it arrives to the shoot in one piece. Companies like KATA, Petrol Bags, and PortaBrace offer professional bags and cases, many tailored specifically to the HDV camcorders on the market. Some models are designed to be used like backpacks, while others feature shoulder straps or carrying handles. The bags provide cushioned support for your valuable camcorder, along with pouches and storage areas for microphones, cables, videotape, and more.

Look Ma, No Tape

Since the late 1950s, videotape has been around in one or more formats. As technology improved, tape formats got smaller and better. While videotape will still be around for some time, it is slowly heading to the land of vinyl records and 8-track tapes. Why? In the digital era, new *tapeless acquisition* technologies provide options that often work better with nonlinear editing solutions. While we will address some tapeless technologies that go beyond HDV in Chapter 7, hard disk drive options specifically designed for HDV are already well established.

FOCUS Enhancements FS-4

FOCUS Enhancements developed the FireStore™ FS-4, which is basically a portable, battery-powered 40, 80, or 120 GB hard disk drive. An IEEE-1394 cable connects the hard drive to the camcorder and video footage is recorded onto a disk drive that clips to your belt. The specifics of the drive are impressive: The hard drive is encased in a shock-resistant plastic enclosure with an internal shock gasket, much like the portable CD players that can absorb small bumps without the disc mistracking. There is a 10-second cache that will prevent any unnecessary interruptions to the signal flow. An additional 8 MB of cache in memory has been standard with a hard drive used to record size-intensive files, such as HDV footage. The speed or revolution of the drive has to be fast—7200 RPM, which is also mandatory when handling the bit flow.

Essentially, the FS-4 is a portable hard drive. It is far more expensive than the standard computer hard drives per gigabyte, but the premium price is for the portability and DC power capability. Once back at your NLE, the FS-4 can be connected directly to your system and the footage seen by the computer as if it's stored on an external hard drive. You can instantly access anything on your "hard drive" without shuttling to find the footage. The time code is displayed as you record the images, and the need for digitizing is eliminated. This allows you to edit your footage more quickly. Erasing the material on the hard drive is also simple and can be done over 1,000 times. Therefore, the initial expense of the recording to the FS-4 winds up being much less than the expense of videotapes in the long run.

Despite its positives, the FS-4 has no external monitor, so there is no way of knowing if your flow of video is being recorded without "glitches." You are basically recording in the dark. The display on your viewfinder or LCD screen informs you what the camera is doing, not what the FS-4 is doing. The FireWire can easily become disengaged from the FS-4, and you don't know if that has happened unless someone is looking at the device. An alarm or a viewfinder function on the unit would be a nice addition.

Finally, because the shooter has no way of knowing if the footage has in fact been recorded, some use the FS-4 as a "double system." In the film days of the 1960s and 1970s, a double system meant that the film was exposed in the camera and the audio portion, usually on 1/4-inch reel-to-reel tape, was recorded on another machine. Therefore, the camera with the film and the audio recorder with its tape were separate items—a double system.

In the same way, tape is inserted in the camera and the FS-4 is connected via a FireWire cable. That way if an "accident" happens with the FS-4, you still have backup footage on the videotape—the double system in use again. If no problems occur, the tape can be erased and the stored footage used instead.

We used the FS-4 on a nautical mission—actually, we had to shoot footage from a canoe. As the breathtaking fall foliage reflected on a still mountain lake, our goal was to record this serene imagery to be used in a travel video. Capturing this ideal setting from land would not have the majesty that the perspective from a canoe would have.

Donning life vests and paddling to the middle of the expansive lake, we used the FS-4 as our capture device mated to a Sony A1. Besides the small whirring sound from the drive, only the rhythmic slapping of the water against our canoe could be heard. With the bow of the canoe in the shot as if seen from the occupant's perspective, we could perform a 300-degree pan to encapsulate all of nature's beauty.

We could have selected tape as our recording medium, but the extended time the FS-4 allowed suited our preferences. The only problem we encountered was with the camera, not the FS-4. If you pan too quickly with the A1U, the images tear slightly as if too much information is presented to the circuits. These "jaggies" are not evident if the shot is extremely slow, but become very pronounced if you move too quickly.

FOCUS Enhancements is not your only tapeless HDV option. Shining Technology, for example, offers its CitiDISK FW1256H family of hard disk recorders, with three models designed to record HDV. The lightweight drives are powered for up to 90 minutes by an internal battery, though an external battery can be used as well for extended shooting. Each unit ships with a belt-carrying pouch, though you can purchase a hot-shoe adapter so it can be attached to your camcorder. Also, Bella Corporation has announced Catapult, a low-cost device that lets you capture DV or HDV footage directly to an iPod™ or other USB drive using a FireWire connection from your camcorder. See **Figure 4.22**.

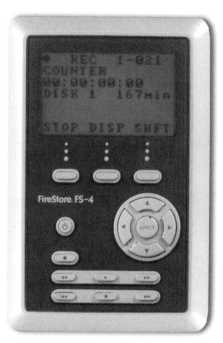

Figure 4.22 The FS-4 from FOCUS Enhancements allows you to record your footage directly to disk, so there's no need to digitize. (Photo courtesy of FOCUS Enhancements)

Serious Magic DV Rack HD

Serious Magic's DV Rack HD is a PC-based tapeless acquisition solution. Ideally installed on a laptop, you can use the computer's internal or external hard drive to store video footage. As shown in **Figure 4.23**, DV Rack HD also includes a full-color monitor, waveform monitor, vectorscope, and audio monitor all in one package displayed on your computer screen.

An HD camera is connected to a computer via FireWire or USB 2.0 connection. The image in the viewfinder is then displayed on your computer's screen and can be scrolled to access a myriad of other monitors and testing equipment (waveform monitor, vectorscope, etc.)

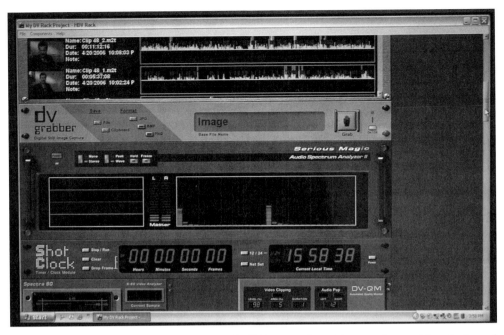

Figure 4.23 Serious Magic's DV Rack HD records video and provides test and measurement information.

You are limited only by the size of your computer's hard drive, so the larger amount of space needed for video files is no longer an issue. The visual and aural information can be monitored while on location. When the shoot is complete, the footage is already on your hard drive and ready to edit. The only downside to this configuration, however, is that you have to rely on your laptop battery if you are shooting at a remote location, and you need to find some way to power the external hard drive. However, at a cost of less than $200, this is your least expensive tapeless solution.

While on a shoot for the government, we used DV Rack HD to record all the footage captured by our camera. Almost all of the material was LCD screens laid out in 16:9—a perfect opportunity to use HDV in its native format. The images on the LCD displays were color radar footage with tiny moving dots representing aircraft in the sky surrounded by thin green bands indicating the terrain. At any given time, up to 2,000 of these "dots" were visible on the monitor. We needed a camera with resolution clear enough to be able to identify these aircraft and the "callout boxes" of information that traveled with them (the aircraft's ID number, altitude, and speed).

The easiest method would have been to obtain an output from the LCD screen and input that directly into our hard drive. Unfortunately, the monitor had S-Video, component, and composite inputs, but no outputs existed—our only option was to record it through a camera. Standard definition would not have had the clarity to make any of the information readable, as text on a computer screen is difficult to read. Luckily, shooting on a progressive LCD monitor produces no scan lines as a CRT does. If air traffic controllers had to read the information on their LCD displays, the video had to capture that same clarity. Studies have proven that an LCD screen is less fatiguing to the eye than a CRT.

The viewfinder on the Sony Z1 was filled with the images from the 16:9 LCD screen. A FireWire cable ran from the camcorder to our Dell® laptop and a Seagate 250 GB external hard drive.

Three hours of screen footage were captured using this process. Because this was a new radar system and was still in the testing phase, it would lock up and all of the display footage would disappear. Our clients could not simply start the program where it stalled; instead, we had to wait for the software to get back to that point (sometimes a 30-minute wait).

With all the footage to date stored on our Seagate drive, the clients would ask us to find the point where the program malfunctioned on the hard drive and we would know exactly where to begin recording again. This immediate accessibility to any footage saved time in determining what information needed to be on the screen at a particular time. Three hours of footage with time code was now immediately available for editing. During the recording process, the time code was also logged so we knew exactly where to locate a specific image, saving additional expense in logging. Without tapeless technology, the shoot would have been much more difficult and expensive.

Having the same benefits as the other options (material is immediately available for editing) it also has one distinct advantage—no moving parts. Where hard drives could fail from an impact or the stylus tracking incorrectly across the surface of the disk, the solid-state option has no parts to stop or bind. Instead, insert the medium and shoot, remove it and edit, over and over up to 10,000 times.

The only deterrent to this method now is the cost. Panasonic has been successful with their P2 cards in their HD camcorder, but the high costs should fall over time.

Tape is still a necessary part of the data acquisition process, but its days are numbered. The potential problems of magnetic interference and tape stretching or shrinking will all disappear in the tapeless environment. As the costs begin to drop, we will be able to shoot footage on a tapeless medium and then toss it in a drawer until we are ready to retrieve the footage or edit it. This may be done thousands of times. If a current MiniDV tape is used more than 10 times, the error rate begins to escalate exponentially.

The Next Generation

As HDV becomes more popular, manufacturers are offering new ways to integrate the format into existing workflows. For example, Miranda offers the HD-Bridge DEC+ converter, which can take an HDV signal and output HD-SDI or downconverted SD-SDI. Convergent Design offers a similar product, HD Connect LE, while DVEO™ offers additional conversion and transport solutions. These products allows HDV users to convert material into other HD (or SD) formats for editing or distribution. Another company, Camplex, has created the Pro X-HD adapter system that allows you to use HDV camcorders as live production cameras.

HDV enthusiasts already have a handful of professional camcorder choices, but manufacturers are already moving forward with the next generation of HDV acquisition. In 2006, JVC announced plans for two new additions to its ProHD line of camcorders, the GY-HD200U and the GY-HD250U (see **Figure 4.24**).

Figure 4.24 The JVC JY-HD250 Camcorder. (Photo courtesy of JVC)

Similar in form to the HD100U, the HD200U is designed to appeal to independent filmmakers, with its 720p/60 acquisition, slow-motion capabilities, and an optional lens adapter that allows the use of 16mm film prime lenses. The HD250U is more of an ENG camcorder, with pool feed video input, HD-SDI output, and a built-in mount for an Anton/Bauer professional battery (in contrast to the smaller batteries that are standard for many HDV camcorders). Plus, the HD250U can be converted into a studio camera using the KY-HD250 studio adapter, which provides connectivity for a 26-pin multicore cable. As a result, a facility can begin to make the transition to HD using existing infrastructure.

The significance of these announcements should not be overlooked. A few years ago, when JVC introduced the first HDV camcorder, the format was dismissed by some critics almost immediately, due in large part to the admitted limitations of the HD10U. Now, the format is well established in the industry, and manufacturers are continuing to introduce new products that address the needs of broadcasters and independent filmmakers. HDV brought high definition to the masses with low-cost camcorders, but the format is now being used with more expensive and specialized products as well.

As the HDV marketplace continues to develop, it will be interesting to see if manufacturers pair the HDV format with camcorders with better imagers. HDV is already offered as a recording choice on XDCAM™ HD camcorders, which use 1/2-inch CCD chips. Plus, optional MPEG-2 recording that conforms to HDV specifications is available with the Grass Valley™ Infinity™ camcorder, which uses 2/3-inch CCD chips. (See Chapter 7 for more details on these alternatives.) Neither Sony nor Grass Valley, however, are emphasizing the HDV standard, arguably because it is still perceived as a low-end HD solution. Whether HDV will be touted in high-end camcorders in the future, rather than primarily relegated to 1/3-inch CCD or 1-CMOS solutions, remains to be seen.

The time for a change has begun and we are still experiencing growing pains. The technology is out there and available—we just have to embrace it.

Points of Interest

- There are a number of accessories that are ideal for HDV camcorders, from filters to camera support systems.

- Tapeless acquisition options are available for HDV camcorders.

- Manufacturers are already creating the next generation of HDV camcorders, as well as solutions to include HDV into existing workflows.

CHAPTER 5

Shooting with HDV

There are several differences between shooting in standard definition and shooting with HDV. For example, HDV's 16:9 aspect ratio provides a much wider field of view, so the framing of your subjects will be unlike that of SD. The depth of field in HDV is diminished, so focus is far more critical. And you need more light for HDV than when shooting in SD.

The reason for this is strange. HDV has more resolution, although the F-stop is essentially the same as any standard definition camera. Because of the improvement in visual quality, the focus is more critical.

Despite these new characteristics, shooting with HDV is worth the re-education, as its dynamic imagery brings new life to your video projects. This chapter will get you familiar with the new aspect ratio, help you prepare for a variety of shooting scenarios, and offer some basic audio tips.

The HDV Difference

Times have changed and so has the terminology. When someone picks up a book on HDV, chances are that person is (for lack of a better term) a "video person," not actually a filmmaker. These people are still making "films" with digital videotape, but they are not filmmakers in the sense that they are using motion picture film cameras (8mm, 16mm, or 35mm).

In order to truly understand HDV, current filmmakers or videomakers must treat the HDV camera as a film camera. Back in the 1970s and early 1980s, video was still in its infancy—film was the only way to get things accomplished. Times have changed, but lighting for film still follows the same rules.

Working with HDV (a catchy title), you must light the scene that same way as you would using a film camera. Video, even HDV, has a four-stop contrast range. That means you have four F-stops difference between the brightest elements (the whites) and the darkest elements (the blacks). Video is compressed and NTSC and PAL televisions could not handle large differences in range between darks and lights.

Motion picture film has a 16-stop contrast ratio—four times that of video. Here is where the difference comes into play. When using the HDV camera and lighting the shot, you want to light as if you have a 16-stop contrast range. Point a light at a black object to make it slightly brighter, or flag or block some light off a white object so it appears gray. Because HDV is sharper than standard definition video, you need that extra light to achieve a sharp focus. Therefore, if you light and expose your HDV image as if you were shooting with a film camera, the recorded image will be better. You still might not see the up to 16 stops range from light to dark, but you will have more depth in your shot.

This brings up a new term, *safe area*. When shooting in HDV or any video format, the shooter must be aware of what will actually appear in the filmed image frame-wise. Almost all HDV cameras have a "safe area" switch that activates a box in your viewfinder and LCD screen that shows a white rectangle border (see **Figure 5.1**).

Figure 5.1 The safe area rectangle displayed on the LCD screen.

When framing, your goal is to keep all of the pertinent action within this area. You will still see on the screen what occurs outside of this bordered area, but use it as a guide. Some televisions overscan, which means they enlarge the televised area, and if action happens outside of the safe area, not all television receivers or monitors might display it accurately. Use it as a guide and after a short period of time you will know to keep the action away from the outer boundaries of the safe area.

Understanding Aspect Ratio

NTSC and PAL share the same aspect ratio, 4:3. These numbers do not pertain to specific measurements in inches, centimeters, or millimeters. Instead they are just given as units. Standard definition television is four units tall by a narrower three units high, or 4:3. This was also called the "Academy Ratio" because it was the same standard aspect ratio used by the Academy of Motion Picture Arts and Sciences from 1932 to 1953. The ratio can also be written as 1.33:1. See **Figure 5.2**.

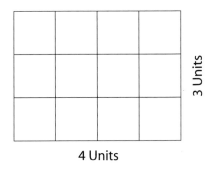

Figure 5.2 Standard definition's 4:3 aspect ratio.

Almost everything is framed in this 4:3 aspect ratio, from home movie film cameras to 35mm and digital still cameras, from older analog camcorders to recent DV models. The format of the projected image on the motion picture screen is different depending on the particular lens used (with or without masking). To be different from television and to try to win back audiences to the larger screen, motion picture producers experimented with a variety of wider aspect ratios. For example, in 1953, the film industry came up with "CinemaScope," which boasted an aspect ratio of 2:35:1. There were a multitude of other aspect ratios around, but most of those were used for only a few films before they died out. Eventually, Hollywood settled on 1.85:1. Super 16mm fits somewhere in the middle of this puddle with its own 1.66:1, which is currently the aspect ratio for films in Europe.

For high definition formats, including HDV, the aspect ratio is 16:9 (1.78:1), a wider aspect ratio that more closely resembles motion pictures than standard television. See **Figure 5.3**. If you prefer using pixels rather than "units" and are editing material in a program like Adobe Photoshop®, the pixel count for SD is 640 × 480, where HDV is 1280 × 720 or 1440 × 1080, depending on your shooting mode.

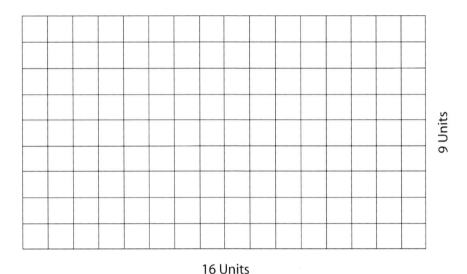

16 Units

Figure 5.3 HDV's 16:9 aspect ratio.

The NTSC broadcast standard, used in North America and Japan, offers 525 lines of horizontal resolution, 60 Hz, and 30 frames per second. The aspect ratio changes when traveling from the United States to Europe. Just as their standard is PAL (Phase Alteration of Line), 625 lines of horizontal resolution, 50 Hz, and 25 frames per second, when shooting in HDV PAL you still have the same 1080i (it is great that the resolution remains the same in both locations), but now the frame rate changes to 50i (60i in the United States) or the film look (or the old PAL standard) 25 frames per second.

The aspect ratio in Great Britain is also 16:9, but it might have been framed differently. It might be a much thinner frame, so the monitor the director uses must have capabilities of displaying both, or gaffer tape would have to be used to mask off the "bands." Knowing this is critical when framing your shot. The microphone might dip into the top of the frame or cables might be seen lying at the bottom if the wrong aspect ratio is selected. Being aware of the system's aspect ratio lines will save headaches and further masking in post.

Directors of photography have been doing this for decades in film: a boom microphone might be easily seen in the viewfinder, but the DP knows that the film will be masked when projected, so the offending item will not be seen by the audience. If you look at the 35mm film frame, the microphone is evident, but on the big screen, no one sees it.

Points of Interest

- NTSC and PAL both support a 4:3 aspect ratio, also written as 1.33:1.

- Motion pictures experimented with a number of aspect ratios, but have generally settled on 1.85:1.

- HDV and other high definition formats feature a 16:9 widescreen format (1.78:1).

Framing for Widescreen

When shooting HDV for the first time, we were impressed at how the frame opened up to allow more visual information. When framing for standard definition's 4:3 for so long, you automatically position your shot so the talent or object is in the most weighted part of the screen. Since that all changes in HDV's 16:9 aspect ratio, how do you effectively frame the shot? Let's start with just one person in the frame and move on from there.

In **Figure 5.4**, we see a young woman framed in HDV's 16:9 aspect ratio. She is sitting in the middle of the frame and looking at the camera. Does this shot look as if it is framed correctly? Yes, because she is looking directly at the camera. This type of framing is successful because it is balanced. If she were not looking at the camera, it would not be balanced (she needs look room). If we were still shooting in 4:3 it might be passable, but not in 16:9.

Figure 5.4 The framing of this shot is balanced with the wider aspect ratio because she's looking at the camera.

If you have watched any movies on the large screen in the theatre, you notice that you rarely see a close-up of someone framed in the middle of the frame. Instead, they reside on one particular side of the frame. Theatrical footage is closer to HDV's 16:9 aspect ratio. Which of the following images is framed correctly—**Figure 5.5** or **Figure 5.6**?

Figure 5.5 The young woman is framed on the left.

Figure 5.6 The young woman is framed on the right.

Actually, either one could be correct. It depends on where she is looking (her eyeline) and if someone else appears in the frame, as if she were having a conversation with a person. If the scene involves cuts between two people talking, it would be best to have one person on the left of the frame and the other on the right. It does not matter which person lives on what side of the frame, as long as you are consistent with the editing.

It is almost as if the framing in **Figures 5.4** and **5.5** just feels right. Again, watch theatrical films and note the framing. If a person is shifting around in the frame, you should naturally have them fall into one of the two examples of framing given above.

The next framing obstacle is finding the natural point for cutting someone off in the frame. As in standard definition, you never want to use natural body cutoff areas like the head, shoulders, waist, and so on. Instead, frame a little above or below these areas for a more natural frame line. Your talent may be on either side of the frame. Look at the following examples in **Figures 5.7**, **5.8**, **5.9**, **5.10**, **5.11**, and **5.12**.

Figure 5.7 A correctly framed long shot (LS).

Figure 5.8 A correctly framed medium long shot (MLS).

Figure 5.9 A correctly framed medium shot (MS).

Figure 5.10 A correctly framed medium close-up (MCU).

Figure 5.11 A correctly framed close-up (CU).

Figure 5.12 A correctly framed extreme close-up (ECU)

To take matters to the next step, how would you frame two people having a discussion? It really depends on the mood of the scene. You may have two people having a heated discussion in the frame, perhaps keeping their distance, not wanting to invade each other's personal space. If this were the case, you can position them at opposite ends of the frame. An example of this is shown in **Figure 5.13**.

Figure 5.13 An angry couple that keeps their distance in the frame emphasizes the space between them.

The opposite would be true if the same two people are having a more tender moment; you want to have less space between them in the frame. Again, you would not want to necessarily frame both people in the center of the frame. Instead, place them off center slightly to the left or the right (as seen in **Figure 5.14**).

Figure 5.14 The argument over, our happy couple shares a tender moment closer together.

We won't say that 16:9 framing should be common sense. Although there is a certain feel to where things should be placed in the frame, it takes practice to get used to its wider aspect ratio. Notice the next five examples in **Figures 5.15** through **5.19**. Each different shot is framed so it appears aesthetically pleasing to the eye. The purpose, as with anything in the frame, is to draw your eye to what you want the viewer to see. Once you have them where you want them, the rest is up to you.

Figure 5.15 A dramatic sunset.

Figure 5.16 Snow-covered branches.

Figure 5.17 Adirondack chairs facing the ocean.

Figure 5.18 A cat taking an afternoon nap.

Figure 5.19 A piece of driftwood on the rocks.

Points of Interest

- Look room (the direction in which the talent is looking) is important in 16:9 shots; avoid centering your subject.

- Just like in SD, don't use natural body cutoff areas (head, waist, etc.) to frame your shot.

- Use the space in the 16:9 aspect ratio to help create mood.

Something's Moving

Now that you know how to effectively frame the shot, how do you show movement within the frame? This is more difficult to explain with still images in a book, but the basic rule is to keep the talent framed in the same area as they move within the frame. Of course, someone could walk from the left side to the right side of the frame in a static shot for a clean entrance and clean exit. However, we are referring to a situation such as an interview, where the person is positioned in the frame but moves and you must reframe the shot.

The most desirable way of achieving this is to mimic what some of the masters have done in the past. Director Robert Altman insisted on having camera movement in every shot in the film. There were never any locked shots where the camera would not pan, tilt, dolly, or zoom. If the camera is always moving, Altman believes, the viewer is pulled more easily into the shot. Just as the human eye is always moving, so should the video frame. Nothing is locked down in real life, so why should we see that in films?

When panning or tilting in the frame, you always want to lead the subject to the next location rather than push them. Allow enough "nose room" (in the front of the frame) so the talent has room to move, and simply go with the flow. While much of this is basic framing direction, the look of the 16:9 frame warrants explaining it again. Obviously, if the person's nose is smack against the edge of the frame, it would be unacceptable in HDV or standard definition. Use your common sense; if the shot looks too confining, it is.

The most effective movement within the camera frame is the slow, creeping zoom in or out. The viewer is slowly pulled in or removed from the shot. We are not talking about drastic moves here; instead, the movement should be subtle, almost imperceptible. Rather than visually seeing the zoom, we should feel it instead.

Let's look at a few specific shooting situations, so we can help you determine the best way to accomplish shooting a particular shot.

The Car Chase

The whole purpose of shooting a sequence such as a car chase is to build tension within the frame for the viewer. The shots need to be rather tightly framed (even in 16:9), and the editing should be fast, with each shot being of a very short duration. We also want to show the viewer as many different angles as possible, cutting between them. How would we do something like this in 16:9?

For the sake of simplicity, we have a good guy and a bad guy, with the good guy driving a white car and the bad guy driving (of course) a black car. We introduce the good guy through a series of close-ups in the car. Because he is driving the car by himself and the steering wheel is on the left (the U.S. version) but on the right as seen through the windshield, we want him framed on the right side of the frame (as seen in **Figure 5.20**). If this were a British movie, the wheel would be on the right and through the windscreen (we used the correct term) he would be sitting and framed on the left.

Figure 5.20 Our good guy is framed behind the steering wheel on the right.

We should shoot a lot of close-ups of the car's interior to aid in editing. We need the hands on the wheel, the brake, the accelerator, and a perspective from behind the driver to show that he is actually piloting the vehicle. The first shot, the hands on the wheel, should be framed on the left side of the frame, because this would be from his point of view. The brake and accelerator shot could be on either side of the frame (not the middle), but the accelerator usually resides on the right and the brake and clutch on the left. We should throw in other shots like the speedometer and extreme close-ups of the talent's face. Again, each shot should be consistent in placement.

We would accomplish the same feat with the bad guy in the other car framed the same way. However, if we wanted the audience to disassociate themselves with the bad guy, we could frame him on the opposite side of the screen. Something would appear not normal with this shot, which could be just enough to throw the audience off. They may not be able to place why they feel uneasy with the shot, but they will (see **Figure 5.21**).

Figure 5.21 The bad guy is framed on the opposite side of the screen.

The shot list should also include lots and lots of exterior shots of the tires squealing, narrowly avoiding other vehicles on the road, scenery whizzing by, and so on. Even though the 16:9 frame allows more information, you want the shots tighter and more claustrophobic when building suspense.

The vehicle could and should travel from one side of the frame to the other—often just panning with the cars as they move may be enough. There are times when you are establishing the vehicles in a new area or location and you would want an extreme long shot. We often see an extreme wide shot with the normal traffic patterns flowing smoothly. At the far left of the frame we see one of the vehicles enter the frame with the other close behind. We have just introduced a new element to the scene (the cars in chase mode) and we want to see how the other vehicles react to the newly added stimulus.

In the same way, we could show what is happening up ahead. In the movie *Speed*, for example, we have a bus that is just trying to stay on the road. The audience knows that if the bus slows down, it blows up. We cut to a shot up ahead where we see (in a wide shot) that the bridge is out. Putting two and two together, we know that the bus is going to arrive at this location and will be in trouble.

You can use the same effect if you show a shot of a traffic jam up ahead—nothing is moving. This will need to be videotaped in extreme telephoto so the distances between the vehicles look as if it is less. The telephoto compresses the image, making it more of a traffic jam than it is. See **Figure 5.22**.

Figure 5.22 A snarled traffic jam could cause problems for our car chase.

Cutting back to the high-speed chase, our good guy and bad guy are not aware of the problem ahead. By cutting from the chase to the jam-up, you create tension. Use the 16:9 aspect ratio for what it does best—showing wide expanses or, in a tight shot, how confined everything is.

The Establishing Shot

HDV's wide aspect ratio is ideal for shooting sweeping vistas with lots of sky. Close-ups have their place, but an establishing shot benefits from the widescreen treatment. Using Canon's XL H1, we shot a majestic waterfall. Beginning with an extreme wide shot of a fast-moving stream, the camera pans right (in the direction of the water flow) to reveal a leaf that was caught in the current. By slowly zooming into this leaf in a medium long shot, we follow its path.

The rushing sound of water is an aural clue that a waterfall is up ahead, as we are still focused on the leaf. Almost immediately, the leaf disappears as it tumbles over the edge of the waterfall. Framed in 16:9, we are only letting the viewer see what we want them to see, deliberately holding back the full force of the waterfall by keeping it out of frame until the last possible moment.

To add a more pronounced effect to the water cascading over the rocks beneath, we shot in 24-frame mode. (Our frame rate choices were 60i, 30, or 24 frames with the Canon XL H1.) Wanting the water to look choppier and more dangerous, the slowest frame rate was selected. This added to the strength of the water, which we wanted for the establishing shot in the piece. Shooting at 30 or even 60 frames would have "smoothed" out the flow of water, and that was not the artistic direction we wanted to take. (See **Figure 5.23**.) Shooting a waterfall in 4:3 simply does not do it justice. Look at the same shot, framed in 4:3 in **Figure 5.24**. Something is missing and the power of the shot is gone.

Figure 5.23 The shot of the mighty waterfall benefits significantly from the 16:9 aspect ratio.

Figure 5.24 The same waterfall in 4:3 loses some of its majesty.

Go West Young Man

Look at any old western—the endless sky and mountains in the distance are always better in widescreen. John Ford used this when shooting *Stagecoach*. We begin with shots of majestic mountains that have been carved by the wind and the vast plain that stretches beneath. Everything is so peaceful and we feel insignificant due to the size of everything in the frame (even in this black-and-white movie). Then, we see something moving, like a tiny speck in the distance. Actually it is more like a cloud of dust. Soon, we realize that it is a stagecoach. But this wide field of view means that, in this wide open space, something as small as a stagecoach is almost impossible to distinguish. This film was not shot in Cinemascope (it was not around yet) but they utilized the wide-angle lens effectively. Just think how this masterpiece would have looked in 16:9.

The very next shot is a medium shot from ground level of the thundering hooves of the horses. But for that first moment in time, we were in awe of the landscape.

Another stimulating use of 16:9 involved using a telephoto lens in the making of the HBO western, *The San Antoine Kid*. Our hero is walking slowly through the desert expanse that runs between Brackettville, Texas, and the Mexican border. This is the same location chosen to shoot the 1960 John Wayne film, *The Alamo*, which was filmed in CinemaScope. We didn't use any of the sets, which are still standing, but the distinct countryside served our purposes.

We decided to lens this film with a 500mm telephoto to drastically reduce the distance our hero was traveling. As he walked toward the camera in extreme telephoto with his saddle over his shoulder, the heat waves behind and in front of him were clearly visible. The human eye does not distinguish this (unless looking through binoculars), but the compression of space makes the waves easily seen in film and video. It was very hot that day when we shot the film, and we wanted the audiences to feel that, too. This just goes to show that you do not always have to shoot 16:9 in wide angle only—telephoto works just as well.

Ah! Nessie

Across the ocean, when we want to establish the massiveness of the moors, or the murkiness of Loch Ness, we select the 16:9 frame. *An American Werewolf in London* used the moor shots effectively by framing the American traveler (soon to be a werewolf) in the middle of a desolate space. He could hear the footsteps and the sounds of the werewolf, but he was seemingly alone on the moors. The camera would zoom in and the shot would become more claustrophobic as his imminent fate approached. Don't show the evil until the last possible moment by keeping it just out of the 16:9 frame.

John Carpenter was a master at this in his first major film, *Halloween*, in 1978. Showing too much empty frame in the widescreen shot makes the viewer wonder if something was lurking at the edge of the frame. Michael Myers always was, but his knife-wielding hand was always just out of frame. Sometimes the camera would come up behind him and we could see the length of the knife's blade glistening in the Panavision frame. This was also an effective use of the "Panaglide," Panavision's version of the successful Steadicam® and Glidecam®.

Politically Correct

Having shot our share of political commercials over the years, shooting another one would seem commonplace. But this time we wanted our candidate to stand out from the pack. Wanting to make a statement, we shot him in HDV with the Sony A1U. Television stations were not yet capable of airing HDV footage, so we had to downconvert (in the camera) to letterbox. Still, no other political spots in the campaign were shot in widescreen.

Framing our candidate on the steps of the state's capital, we shot from below to make him appear more dominant in the frame, as if he were larger than life. The sharp horizontal lines of the steps in the background made this an appealing shot. He was framed on the left and would be looking in to the right until he turned to the camera and spoke. Still on the left side, he would deliver his statement as the camera slowly zoomed in to a full close-up.

Because the Sony HDV was so small, no one knew we were shooting a political ad. Our two-person crew and small camcorder attracted no attention. When the letterbox spot was finished, our candidate actually got the most votes. Was it because our candidate was really that good, or because our spot was different from the rest?

Shakespeare in the Studio

In a pilot program for PBS, we embarked on getting junior high school students more interested in the plays of William Shakespeare. PBS shoots much of its original material in HD. We used the JVC JY-HD100U shooting in 720p/24. Our location was a TV studio with a black curtain backdrop (we wanted a void), with the talent sitting on a stool in the middle of the room.

The first actor was a blonde-haired woman who recited a sonnet from *Hamlet*. Framed in a medium shot from slightly above the waist, she wore a black blouse and black slacks. Before we get any further into the framing, however, we have to address lighting. After all, how do you make someone stand out in the frame when they are wearing the same color clothing as the rear wall?

The obvious answer is to use a backlight to clearly separate the talent from her surroundings. Using the lighting grid in the studio, a 1K fresnel was focused on her head and shoulders. With a half scrim (a screen on the bottom half of the light source) on the top of the fresnel, we blasted the light on her. Dark objects absorb light and lighter objects reflect—her hair would be the reflector and her blouse would be the absorber. The scrim was placed in the top of the light, effectively removing two stops of light from her blonde hair. If her hair color had been darker, we probably would not have used the scrim. More of the light (without scrim) was used to separate her shoulders from the background. Having a slight ring or rim of light around her shoulders is often all you need for a slight "pulling away" from the background.

Our F-stop was low enough that the black curtain was barely visible, so she appeared as if she were in a void. Of course, a backlight alone will not do justice, especially in three-point lighting. To keep the heat at a minimum, we used fluorescent lights as the key and fill. The key was a four-bank 55-watt, tungsten-balanced, cool source, and the fill was a two-lamp unit, both from Ikan Corporation.

Bathed in a gentle cool light, we still needed the woman to appear warmer and friendlier to the small masses viewing her. Using the advanced menu on the JVC camcorder, we played with the color saturation of her face and made it warmer by raising the level of the skin tones to plus two. We had other features like skin softening, which blurs some of the age lines but usually looks artificial. Shooting in 24p, we had a film-like look to the woman in black.

Any director of photography worth his salt will always choose an F-stop and stick with it, raising or lowering the level of the lights until it hits the mark. Our standard has always been F4 and that's what we chose for this shoot. With the four-bank light being five feet away and the same distance on the other side for the fill light, we had an even F4 on the talent, her blouse was an F2.8 (because it was absorbing light), and a one-stop difference from her face was suitable. **Figure 5.25** illustrates our set-up.

Figure 5.25 We used three-point lighting in the studio for our HDV shoot.

The framing of this video did not require much movement in the frame; instead, it was the framing of the shots that was different. When first establishing her speaking, we used the traditional long shot, medium shot, and close-up. But since we were producing a video that had to entertain junior-high-school students—and interest them in something like Shakespeare—we had to do something that was slightly offbeat.

The camera was still locked down on a tripod, but the director wanted unusual shots, such as extreme close-ups of her mouth, eyes, face, and hands as she gestured. Many times when we were shooting, her hand would leave the frame, we'd use a diagonal tilt from her mouth to her eyes, or we'd use an extreme close-up of some part of her face. This is not traditional filmmaking, but when cut together you have a visually appealing piece of video.

There is no right or wrong way to shoot this, but the use of HDV with the wider aspect ratio allows you even more latitude when filling the frame. The mouth could be on the far left and then, after a cutaway, be on the extreme right. We were told to have fun with the shots and be unconventional, and that's precisely what we did. You cannot be told what to shoot in situations such as this; we just used the 16:9 frame to our advantage and got unusual shots that cut together without appearing disjointed. This was an excellent opportunity to practice with the HDV frame and see what worked and what did not.

Points of Interest

- Three-point lighting is still effective for HDV.

- Use the wider aspect ratio to hide what may be lurking just out of frame.

- Currently HDV (the letterbox frame) is not the norm and it will attract attention.

Shooting Nature—Naturally

High definition video has been a boon for nature filmmakers. In the past, they would shoot miles of film to get that "perfect shot," rush to have the film processed and, more recently, transferred from the original negative to digital tape. With HDV on the market, these same shooters can record hours of tape at a fraction of the cost of one core (roll) of 16mm film.

No matter what type of creature you have as a subject, shooting nature is always unpredictable. You have no idea what the subject is going to do next (much like children). The best you can do is to just be patient and record everything—you have up to an hour in most MiniDV formats, so the only time you stop the camera is to change tapes.

We were stalking the male hummingbird recently and, because they are so skittish and flighty (sorry), we had to record quite a few tapes to capture the shot we wanted. Using the JVC again, we quickly encountered an electronic "stamina" problem. In 720p/24, the images from the Fujinon lens look great. However, the camera comes with an on-board battery that lasts only 20 minutes when using the flip-out LCD screen. If you use the color viewfinder, your running time is increased to about 75 minutes. This is unacceptable for a marathon nature shoot.

JVC recommends using an Anton/Bauer brick battery that will give you hours of performance. Of course, there is always the AC route but, alas, most hummingbirds are found outdoors in the wild, not conveniently located near a power outlet. A portable generator would create the same problem as older 16mm film cameras: loud noise. In order to videotape the elusive hummingbird, you must be very patient and still when they are feeding. Because their metabolism is so fast and their wings beat hundreds of times a minute, these little delicacies burn themselves out very quickly. It took us more than an hour at one particular feeder to get the male specimen we wanted.

To make matters worse, there were four possible feeder tubes from which to choose—we had no idea where the hummingbird was going to land, if at all. Because males are also territorial, if they see another male in the vicinity, they will attack them. We wanted to show grace and beauty, not bloodthirsty melee.

In order to conserve the battery, we used the viewfinder only and stopped the tape when the hummingbirds were not around. When a male did come into view, which is evident from the red band around his throat, we hit the record button. Doing a slow creep-in zoom without moving our bodies, we captured the shot you see in **Figure 5.26**.

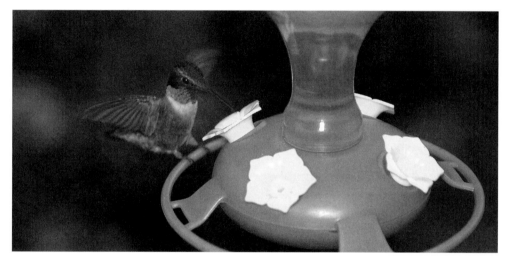

Figure 5.26 A male hummingbird feeding as captured by the JVC JY-HD100U.

While we were out "shooting" hummingbirds, we also collected other cutaway shots of animals to use throughout the documentary. Because we were at the whim of the hummingbirds, we thought we should have some other HDV footage while we were there. Squirrels are natural clowns and are entertaining when trying to feed. On any shoot, it's better to get too much footage than not enough (see **Figure 5.27**).

Figure 5.27 A squirrel in its natural habitat—the backyard.

Of course, hummingbirds and squirrels are docile and relatively harm-less. If your targets include lions, tigers, bears, or other potentially dan-gerous prey, it's best to use your most telephoto setting and remain at a safe distance. The camera will make almost no noise and, unless you are talking, you should not disturb the animals. Also, never wear strong colognes; humans have a natural scent already strong enough that most animals can detect it immediately. It may sound unsanitary, but rubbing your face, hands, and clothes with dirt will help mask your scent and you might get closer to the target. (If you are in a relationship, make sure you clean up after the shoot or you will not get very close to your significant other's target!)

It's About Time

Still dealing with nature videography, time lapse in HDV allows you to capture the event over an extended period of time. Although the JVC GY-HD100U does not offer this feature, sometimes just recording a few seconds of footage at a time will work. On another nature quest, for example, we used HDV to document the growth cycle of song sparrows from egg until they leave the nest.

We were not able to build an enclosure for the nest and the camera; instead, we found a shrub four feet from the ground with the makings of a nest. In the wild, you could insert the camera into the shrub and activate it remotely, but we did not want to disturb the mother or her siblings. We decided to frame the nest on the left side of the frame. We videotaped just a few minutes once every eight hours, only when the mother left the nest. **Figure 5.28** shows our first encounter after the eggs were layed and two had hatched.

Figure 5.28 A song sparrow's nest with two occupants awake.

Figure 5.29 Still pink, but semi-awake.

Only eight hours later, both birds were slightly bigger, but still in the same position. (See **Figure 5.29**). The next morning, or actually sometime during the night, the rest of the family hatched wearing their pink underwear. (**Figure 5.30**). Growing voraciously, their mouths are open and ready for food as seen in **Figure 5.31**.

Figure 5.30 Every bald member accounted for.

Figure 5.31 Feed me!

Again, eight hours goes by and they are growing quickly (**Figure 5.32**). When morning arrived, they all had joined the "Hair Club for Men," illustrated in **Figure 5.33**. That afternoon as seen in **Figure 5.34**, the birds were ready to leave the nest. This was our last video of the family.

Figure 5.32 Is it getting crowded in here?

Figure 5.33 Eyes still closed, but it won't be long.

Figure 5.34 Bird nest for rent soon.

Points of Interest

- Shooting nature is unpredictable, so be ready for a long production day.

- Have plenty of tape available; you'll need it.

Just Say I Do

One of the biggest potential markets for HDV is event video, such as recitals, bar and bat mitzvahs, concerts, plays, and sporting events. At this time, the most popular use for HDV is weddings, an industry which has always been on the cutting edge of new video technology. For example, this market was the first to market DVD-Rs as the end result rather than VHS tape.

Couples are spending a few dollars for these events, and the immediacy of video allows the wedding ceremony to be viewed at the reception immediately afterward. So, how do you make the transition from SD to HDV when most newlyweds will not have HDV playback equipment?

This will be discussed in more detail in Chapter 6, but for talking purposes, let's say you ask the couple if they want their wedding shot in HDV. Usually, their response will be, "I don't know," or "What's that?" When you started offering DVDs to your clients, they were likely already familiar with the format. "How great would it be to see our wedding on DVD?" Easy sell.

The next logical step is high definition and you need to sell this new technology. Here are some strategies that have been successful for us. You can explain the wider aspect ratio. Maybe they've checked the HDTVs at a local electronics store. If either of them is a sports fan, perhaps they've seen the Super Bowl or another contest in HD. Even if they haven't seen HD, you then tell them that HDV provides sharper and clearer images than what they see on their current TV sets and it will fill a widescreen picture. If they do not have a 16:9 set, downconverting it to letterbox will still look professional. To help make them aware of the advantages, we'll often project a 16:9 wedding (downconverted) on the projector in our studio. On a 10-foot screen, they immediately get the idea that their wedding video will be just like watching a movie (hopefully without the chase scene). Again, we will discuss this in more detail in Chapter 6, but they would receive a downconverted, 16:9 wedding video on DVD.

Is this type of video framed or lit differently? Most assuredly so. We always find it exciting to shoot the bride getting ready in 16:9 black and white. Much like an old still photograph, the timeless quality of a softly lit black-and-white image is intoxicating. **Figure 5.35** illustrates how we shot Crystal's preparations in black and white.

Figure 5.35 A future bride in black and white.

Once the couple is introduced to each other at the ceremony, here is where we choose to frame the 16:9 shots differently. When shooting from behind the couple, we have each of them on separate sides of the frame. They are not a union yet; as the ceremony moves farther along, we will come in closer so they are in the center of the frame.

If you are fortunate enough to videotape from the front, extreme close-ups of their faces capture the emotions of the day. Tilt down to show the rings—still in close-up—and pull out to show the rest of the wedding party. Sometimes this is the only opportunity to videotape the entire party in 16:9, especially if the wedding party has several people involved. **Figure 5.36** shows the happy couple during the ceremony.

Figure 5.36 Our happy couple poses after exchanging their vows.

Outdoor candid shots between the ceremony and reception lend themselves to be shot in 16:9 by framing trees, ponds, or other structures in
the shot (as seen in **Figure 5.37**). Stretch limousines will look exceedingly
long in 16:9, and unless you want that fact noted, don't shoot low-angle
shots of the limo.

Figure 5.37 Our couple in a relaxed setting.

The reception is where most videographers run into trouble in HDV. For
reasons never cleared through the wedding videographer, far too often the
couple and their guests congregate in a room that is dark, intimate, and lit
by candlelight. This type of footage is what HDV hates. You have several
options here—some may keep the mood while others will destroy it.

If you want to keep the mood intact, you may open your iris (the JVC
opens to F1.6, which is pretty fast), but your depth of field (the area within the frame remains in focus) will be very narrow, an inch or two at best.
In HDV, you already know focus is critical. If you are even slightly soft
when shooting, the romantic image will be blurry when viewed on anything bigger than your viewfinder.

We find it helpful to use JVC's Focus Assist, which rings the image with blue lines, also known as zebras. These zebras are the same indicators used when making sure your video luminance (brightness) is not exceeding the video's parameters. With the focus assist on, roll the focus barrel or ring back and forth through the focusing point until you find something that is acceptable. Focus for the eyes and not the nose—eyes are the gateway to the soul, but no one really has much to say about the nose. Some focus while shooting, but we usually do it before the camera rolls because we always give the couple all of the footage in addition to an edited package. Sony's FX1 and Z1 have a similar feature for assisting in focusing.

Try to get as close to the couple as possible without having the wide-angle lens distort. The wider your lens, the greater your depth of field—this is important when shooting at F1.6. But do not make the bride look as if she is in a fishbowl.

Another option is to increase the video gain. The side effect of this is that it adds noise to the image by making the numerous pixels easier to see. At −18 dB you have three extra stops of light, but enough grain particles to fill hundreds of cereal bowls. This would not be our favorite option, although sometimes just increasing it one stop to −3 dB may be enough to brighten the scene.

The last option that does not cause too much trouble is to decrease the shutter speed of the camera. Most cameras are set at 1/60 of a second. To gain extra stops, we have shot in 1/30, which is one stop, and 1/15, which opens two stops. There are side effects with this scenario, most notably the slower your shutter speed, the more strobing occurs with fast-moving objects. Sometimes just someone dancing at 1/15 is enough to strobe. As an effect once in a while it is not too bad, but do not use it all the time.

You can always explain to the couple that the room is extremely dark (they may not be aware of it because they have other things than your video on their minds), and then ask if you could turn the lights up slightly to increase the clarity of your image. It never hurts to ask—the worst they can say is no. But it's how they say it that hurts. We have had about half say yes and half say no. Rather than raising three stops immediately, have the person on the lights increase them gradually, if possible, so the dancers and merrymakers are not aware of it happening.

Our least favorite choice here is to use an on-camera light, which makes you look as if you are shooting some sleazy news event where the couple is in the searchlight and everyone else is dancing in a void. You can set up lights at the corners of the room and bounce them off the ceiling, but some drunken guest is bound to stagger into at least one of them and knock it on the floor.

If lighting is an issue, you must address it. If you keep your mouth shut and the couple cannot make out Aunt Bertha and Uncle Henry doing the cha-cha, they will complain. We learned early on that this is critical and needs to be brought to their attention. You are not asking them how they want the shots framed, just if you can have a little more light to—use these words—"get a sharper, clearer image." Do not mention exposure or stops. You may think you sound cool, but they are busy and have little time to be interrupted with questions. They will want their images as sharp and clear as they can be.

Backtracking, the same thing applies to the church, synagogue, or other location of the wedding ceremony. Always get there before time, attend the rehearsal (so you know where people are going to stand and who may be blocking you), and check your exposure and focus. Many churches are vast caverns that suck up all available light, but if you are shooting a spring or summer wedding, you might have enough light filtering in through the windows. Then, frame up your shots and let the world of 16:9 come alive.

Finally, it makes good sense to play back some of your footage to make sure you *have* footage. This one-time event won't be repeated—no footage means no payday (and yes, this has happened). Always be sure you are recording and that you have extra videotape on site in case of a problem.

Points of Interest

- In poorly lit receptions, you can raise the gain, lower your shutter speed, or add light.
- Use telephoto for intimate moments and wide-angle lenses for larger group shots.

Corporate Shoots

When shooting real estate in HDV, any building will look better in 16:9. Exteriors lend themselves to this aspect ratio and even small, claustrophobic rooms look larger with a wide-angle lens. You are not deceiving the buyer by shooting this way; instead, you are using the tools at hand more effectively.

We were called upon to videotape an ice cream parlor that was for sale. We have shot numerous businesses before, and this one did not seem any different until we arrived at the location. The original owner was the "Shoe King" of Lancaster, and he had decided to build his domicile in the mid-1940s to resemble a large shoe. (See **Figure 5.38**). Getting as close as possible and still framing it on the left in HDV, the deep, blue sky added to the majesty of the abode. You could say it had a lot of . . . sole.

Figure 5.38 A really big shoe (sorry Mr. Sullivan).

When you have miles of chrome that you must illuminate and shoot seductively on a Harley-Davidson® motorcycle, 16:9 can add to the impact. Not wanting to use hard, directional light on chrome (it just reflects back into the camera), we chose to diffuse the source with umbrellas. Two 750-watt Lowel Omnis were used at the left and the right of the frame to raise the ambient light level.

Because the Harley is also bathed in jet black paint, we needed illumination on those surfaces so they would register on the camera. A third 750-watt Lowel Omni was scrimmed and placed six feet from the body of the bike. Two 1000-watt Lowel Totas were gelled with rose gel and bounced off the back wall. The red color complemented the black and chrome bike as well as the red tool boxes in the garage. **Figure 5.39** shows our setup. The model, also dressed in black leather, straddled the bike. The black leather on her absorbed the light without overexposing her skin.

Figure 5.39 My, what nice chrome you have.

Another corporate video was shot, this time with the JVC GY-HD100U, to make the viewer more aware of what a candy factory actually does. Of course, we shot B-roll of the factory floor itself, with its noisy machines clanking along. But anytime you shoot an interview, you must remove your subject from that environment into a far quieter space.

Move your CEO, tool maker, press operator, or whoever your interview subject is to a quiet office. Every person in a corporate video should be identified on screen, no matter who they are. Make sure you get the correct spelling of their name and title for the graphics. Framing may be seen in **Figure 5.40,** with the first person being on the right or left of the frame. It is wise to alternate sides if cutting between interviews and will be more visually pleasing. If your space is limited and only one side works, try using cutaways of something between the interviews.

Figure 5.40 A nicely framed interview subject.

When shooting in the factory, let your 16:9 frame lead the flow along the conveyor belt. If you go against the flow, the viewer will perceive something wrong and the shot will not be as effective. Slow zooms in and out will break the monotony of pans. Try getting extreme close-ups as often as possible. Use the detail that HDV allows, making sure everything is sharply focused.

When shooting landscapes, you may want to shoot more of the sky to fill your 16:9 frame. You still need to see the horizon, but if the light streaming down through the clouds is what you are after, show just enough of the ground to establish a location. (See **Figure 5.41**.)

Figure 5.41 It's all in the clouds.

Backlighting, as mentioned earlier, is when the strongest light source is coming from behind the subject and the foreground object becomes a silhouette. In HDV, with its lower contrast range than film, it is more difficult to achieve and well worth the effort if pulled off effectively as seen in **Figure 5.42**.

Figure 5.42 Backlit grass in silhouette.

There are hundreds of other possibilities for shooting and lighting in HDV's 16:9. Frame the shots correctly with enough head room and make sure you have enough light on the set to achieve a proper exposure. It never hurts to check your focus often—if someone leans back in a chair, that may be enough to require a refocus. Frame the shot with enough room around the frame, achieve a proper exposure and lock it, and use the camera's focus assist to keep your images from going soft.

Points of Interest

- Use the 16:9 aspect ratio to accentuate the size of a building.

- Conduct your corporate interviews away from busy, noisy work areas.

Closing Thoughts

The JVC HD100U got more than its far share of mention in this chapter. Chapter 6 will focus on some of the other great offerings in the HDV world from Sony and Canon, and how they work with nonlinear editing.

CHAPTER 6

HDV Post

In this chapter we can start to put everything together. You have used your HDV camera and recorded quite a bit of footage on your MiniDV tapes. Now comes the logging, sorting, and editing process.

Here we will discuss the technical considerations needed for the post process. including:

- What kind of nonlinear editing (NLE) system do you need to edit the footage?

- Will your computer's processor and memory be enough to handle the load?

- How much storage capacity should your hard drive contain?

- Will you be editing natively in HDV or will you be downconverting and posting in standard definition?

- Exactly how do you get HDV footage into your computer?

Also, you must make some creative choices in the posting process regarding which shots will have the most impact, how complicated or simple the edit should be, and whether compositing original music, graphics, and so on will be needed. You will also need to determine who your viewing audience will be and tailor the program accordingly.

Finally, we will discuss the content delivery options:

- Will the final product be in standard definition to air on television?

- Should it be in HDV for a presentation to a large audience via a video projector?

- Do you need two versions, one standard definition and one HDV to prepare for an HD future?

- Will the end result fit on DVD or will it need Blu-ray™ or HD-DVD?

All these questions will be answered in this chapter. The final determination will still be yours; we simply want to provide you with all of the necessary options.

Please Consider This

A sense of relief usually comes when you have shot the last frame of your epic and the crew has wrapped. But, now that the production has been completed, you must immediately begin thinking about what happens next—post production.

During the course of your shoot, we're sure you have at least been thinking about what you want in post. Since the final scene has been shot, now is the time to make the decision. The first decision is going to be the hardest, in our opinion.

Let's say you have just completed a 60-minute MiniDV tape with HDV footage of your client's commercial product. You chose to shoot in 1080i HDV and all you must do now is rewind the tape, digitize it, and begin editing. Your first question is "Do I edit natively in 1080i, create a 30-second spot, export it to tape, and give it to the local cable channel?"

This may work a short time from now but, as of this writing, very few stations will be able to air your 1080i footage (or your 720p footage, for that matter). But does that mean you cannot edit natively in HDV? No, not necessarily. We will address that issue shortly. The other option is to downconvert the footage and have a letterboxed version for air. This will make the TV stations happy, but your beautiful HDV footage is now presented in plain old NTSC or PAL.

Let's look at another scenario. A colleague of ours at the university wanted to shoot a feature in 720p using JVC's HD100U. He shot four MiniDV tapes worth of material (his first weekend shoot) and we asked him how he was going to post the video. He told us that, if edited natively, only one NLE system that he had would work. That meant the students who were doing the shot logging would have to come to his house and digitize all four hours of footage. His end product would be an HDV master for film festivals. If he chose the other route, he would attach the JVC to another MiniDV deck, dub the HDV footage to a squeezed standard definition tape, and have the students log the footage on his hard drive at the school. That would keep his students from eating all the food in his refrigerator, but the original time code could be different on the SD dubs, lengthening the process. The squeezed footage could still be transformed at the end. The end result came down to storage space. His hard drive was not big enough to handle a feature film in native HDV.

Until recently, Avid could not handle HDV editing if you shot in 720p/24. Shooting in 30 fps was not an issue with 720p, but that elusive 24p was not a happy camper. If during the importing process the user selected 23.97 frames progressive, the Avid system would accept the footage (much like

NTSC is not really 30 fps but actually 29.97). This was not explained at the time so our client had to learn this the hard way. The moral of this story is to be specific on your frame rate—23.97 is 24p.

Real Editing—Save the Last Mac for Me

Before you begin the process of post in standard definition or HDV, you must make sure your equipment is up to the task. The first thing to look at is the computer you will be using (the software comes in later). In the Macintosh® world, you have a few options. Currently the Macintosh G5 is strong and fast enough to edit HDV files. G4s do not quite have the processor speed. G5s in tower, desktop, or laptop with operating system OS X or greater (Panther® and all of the other cool names) have processor speeds that are fast enough to handle the larger files. Some even prefer to use dual processor Macs, which will accomplish the task in even less time. As of this writing, Macs were incorporating Intel® chips (a PC's processor), which brings the speed up even higher.

The second item that your Macintosh needs is a FireWire (IEEE-1394) port to get your HDV footage into and out of the computer. Macs have both FireWire 400 and 800 ports, with the 800 being far superior. You don't want your transfer process to "clog" so if your Mac can handle FireWire 800 (and you have the cable), that method is preferred. USB 2, which is light-years faster than USB 1 and faster than FireWire 400, has not been selected over FireWire for video editing. This is probably why most manufacturers supply FireWire cables instead of USB 2 cables with the cameras.

The third thing you need is memory. The old adage is true; you can never have too much memory. A minimum for HDV is 512 megabytes, with most software programs recommending at least two gigabytes. A year ago, having that much memory was considered overkill.

Being PC

In the PC world, things are not that much different. A Pentium® 4 processor is recommended (with lesser Pentiums not really being readily available) running Windows® XP Home or Professional. The processor speed must be greater than 2 GHz with those approaching 4 GHz being best. A dual processor never hurts either, and the memory requirement is the same as that of the Macs—two gigs are best. FireWire 400 is standard, with a few PCs having FireWire 800, but the 400 will get you by.

Now that you have a computer (Mac or PC) that is up to speed (pardon the pun), you need to look at storage next.

How Much Room Do I Have?

The obvious difference between PCs and Macs is that the hard drive must be formatted for that computer (a Mac drive must be formatted for Mac and a PC for PC). The drives themselves may be identical, but once you format them for one computer, they will remain that way until they are reformatted. Before we get too deep into the formatting, let's look at a few other things first.

The name brand of the drive is important—there is some cheap junk out there. Stay with a name you have heard of: Maxtor®, Western Digital, LaCie, Seagate, and so on. Everyone has a favorite manufacturer and most have horror stories about the trouble they had with "X" brand. Get the biggest drive (capacity) you can afford. Anything smaller than 100 gigabytes will be too small for HDV work of any magnitude. Drives with 300 and 500 gigabytes are popular and portable (in external configuration) and anything up to a terabyte is somewhat affordable. (See **Figure 6.1**).

Figure 6.1 A Seagate 300 gigabyte external hard drive.

Internal drives are far cheaper than external drives, but you are paying for portability with an external drive. Once you have your "really big drive," look into the revolutions per minute or RPM. A hard drive is like an old record player (remember those?). A stylus (the needle) writes information onto a disk (the record) and the faster the disk spins, the more information will flow onto it without clogging it up or slowing it down. With 25 Mbps of information flowing through the FireWire onto the hard drive in HDV, the disk better be moving quickly.

A speed of 7,200 RPM is the absolute slowest speed you should consider. Some laptop internal drives are 5,000 RPM, which is fine for recording word-processor files but not larger, more complex video files. Drives with 10,000 and 15,000 RPM are far better, but they are quite expensive (at this writing). Now that you have the big three factors in your hard drive (RPM speed, name product, and enough gigabytes), let's look at formatting.

The PC offers two options in formatting: FAT32 and NTFS. Most new hard drives come preformatted from the factory in FAT32, which is fine for word processing and data files, but not video. We are not saying FAT32 will not handle video files, but you will have issues, especially with HDV files. Instead, right click on "My Computer," select "Manage," select "Disk Management" and change the FAT32 to NTFS. A quick format on a 500 gigabyte drive will take about two minutes.

With NTFS the computer will store your video and audio files wherever it needs to and you may access them later. This brings up another issue called maintenance. You should *defragment* your hard drive often. As information is sent from your camera to the drive, the computer puts it in various places where it finds space—rarely together. When you recall that information, the computer will find it quickly even though it may be in several locations on the disk. After a period of time, these old, excess fragments build up and slow down the speed of your editing. You will be aware of this when you start encountering funky problems while trying to edit.

When this happens, save your file in your software program, right click on "My Computer," select "Manage," choose "Defragment" and select the drive you would like to defragment. This does not mean you must start defragmenting immediately. Choose the "analyze" tab and in a few moments you will be told if you need to defragment and what percentage the drive is defragmented. Depending on the size of your drive (there's that size thing again), it could take hours to defragment the drive. Once you start defragmenting, your editing on that drive will stop until the process is done.

If your drive needs to be defragmented, do it and your performance will increase. It does not matter if you are at the end of your project, just beginning, or in the middle, the defragmenting process will not hurt or destroy any files. It's just putting them together without having fragments all over the place. Make sure your editing file is not open when you begin defragmenting. Just close the program and open the defragmenter.

There are two ways around this to make your life happier—one way is to get a RAID array (random access internal drives). As information is sent from the HDV camera to RAID drives, it is placed on several different drives at the same time. That way, if one part of the drive fails, you still have your footage elsewhere that can be used. This is the best and most accurate way of storing video files, but it is also the most expensive. A RAID drive costs four times what the same size standard hard drive costs. These drives do not require defragmenting as often.

The other solution is with the Apple® folks. In Mac Land, there is no FAT32 or NTFS. Just install the drive, format it for Macintosh and you are ready to go. Defragmenting a drive is still necessary, but we have found you do not need to do so quite as often. But again, if your files are stored on a Macintosh hard drive, you cannot open them with your PC.

Now you should have everything you need to know about what type of computer to use and what is available. Next, we must find a software program that is compatible with HDV.

Software, Software Everywhere

As you read early on, HDV footage is different from standard definition AVI or Mac's QuickTime files. When HDV footage is entered into a computer, the file is converted to the MPEG-2 format. If you connected your HDV camera via FireWire to your computer and opened the software program, if it does not support HDV, it probably will not even recognize that the camera is attached. This is a new format and editing MPEG video is tricky. The transport stream of MPEG is not commonly supported by desktop tools. Therefore, a new approach had to be devised.

One of the problems of MPEG video editing is that this format compresses large numbers of consecutive frames together as a grouping to take advantage of the similarities between adjacent frames. Because this data is compressed, you cannot access individual frames directly. Sometimes you may be able to edit at boundaries but that is not accurate enough.

In order to solve this dilemma, more sophisticated MPEG tools had to be developed to support frame-accurate editing that would provide this access to individual frames by decoding the entire group and then re-encoding them together again. If this isn't done correctly, these recompressed blocks of data do not know where they belong and end up as digital artifacts (digital artifacts are bad news). These are the kind of artifacts that will never be worth anything to scientists.

JVC, with their defunct HD10U came out with *MPEG Edit Studio™ Pro*, which offered two video tracks, transitions, audio mixing, and rolling titles. You could output to MPEG-2 standard definition or HDV. With a list price of $1,800, it was expensive—but it worked. This was helpful, because at 720p with MPEG-2 compression the flow rate was only 19 Mbps instead of the usual 25 Mbps, which standard definition digital video uses.

Not listed in any particular order, here are some of the software programs that testify that they are HDV capable (as of this writing). The list includes but is not limited to:

- Sony Vegas® (*www.sony.com/mediasoftware*)

- Adobe Premiere Pro 2 (*www.adobe.com*)

- Avid Xpress Pro HD (*www.avid.com*)

- Apple Final Cut Pro HD 5 (*www.apple.com*)

- Ulead® Media Studio Pro 8 (*www.ulead.com*)

We are sure there are other NLE programs out there, but this is just a sample listing of some of the more popular choices. Later in this chapter we will step you through the editing phase of three projects, each using a different NLE program and a different HDV camcorder, and discuss the strengths and weaknesses.

Some of these choices are easier to make than others. With the Sony HDV cameras (the FX1, A1, or Z1) you have more options: edit natively in 1080i or downconvert to one of the three options addressed in Chapter 4. If using the JVC, your options are limited with Apple's Final Cut Pro HD—this version of the software will not edit footage natively with the HD100U. Your only option here is to output in squeezed standard definition. If using Avid Xpress Pro HD or Adobe Premiere® Pro 2 you have more options (native or conversion to standard definition). With Canon's XL H1 you can use any program for native editing because the footage is in 1080, or you still have the SD squeezed option.

Project One—The World's in a Spot

The first project we will discuss is a high-end television commercial that was shot with the Sony Z1. We chose this camera because of all of the downconversion options it incorporates in shooting for post (editing 1080i natively, letterbox standard definition, squeezed, and edge cropped). Our choice for editing was Adobe's Premiere Pro 2.

We reread Chapter 5 of this book and lit the sets as if we were shooting with a film camera with its higher contrast range. The last commercials we shot for this client used Super 16mm film and therefore the transition from film to HDV was a smooth one (the end result would be letterbox, much like Super 16mm's 1.66-to-one aspect ratio). See **Figures 6.2** and **6.3** for illustrations from this shoot.

Figure 6.2 On the set with the Sony Z1.

Figure 6.3 An actual frame from the completed spot.

The best way to cause the viewer to identify with the talent on the screen is to shoot in close-up so you can see their eyes. Eyes are the gateway to the soul and this is one way of trying to see inside. The two attorneys in the commercials wanted to appear believable, genuine, and willing to listen. Their offices were warmly lit with soft Fresnel lights and Chimeras, and three-point light was imperative.

We began by shooting testimonials of their clients saying how these attorneys had changed their lives for the better. The testimonials were also shot in close-up with Sony's Zeiss lens on the Z1 slowly creeping in on the talent's face. Modeled with a key, fill, back, and hair light, the crisp edge of HDV was toned down using the CineFrame 24 (film-like speed) and skin-softening feature of the Sony. A low-contrast filter could also have been used to soften the HDV image, but we did not want to tone down that much and chose to let the camera do it instead with its internal circuitry, gamma gain, and skin-softening feature.

Because we were shooting interviews, the amount of tape used was considerable. Although the end product was only 30 seconds, we could not tell the clients what to say. Instead, we had to phrase the questions asked of them in such a way that the answers we were looking for would be given.

When using the Sony or the Canon, both manufacturers recommend the Sony Digital Master Series Tape PHDVM-630DM. The label on the box clearly states that the tape is "designed for HDV," and provides 63 minutes of tape per cassette. As we discussed in Chapter 2, this tape is more expensive than standard MiniDV tape, but its dual-layer tape formulation is designed to provide fewer dropouts and errors (digital artifacts) than standard DV tape. You are using an HDV camera; it deserves a better, more reliable tape.

We could have shot in Sony's DVCAM format, but we chose HDV/DV mode. We have not noticed any quality differences between DVCAM and DV's SP speed, so that speed was selected.

Once the five tapes were recorded, we were ready to begin the post process. As mentioned early in this book, we often use Serious Magic's DV Rack HD as a production tool. Although we recorded all of the footage on tape in the camera, a FireWire cable connected the Z1 to our Sony Vaio® Pentium 4 laptop. The footage could be captured as MPEG-2 files on a Maxtor 160 gigabyte external hard drive. If we chose to, we could immediately begin editing because the files were already converted to MPEG-2 and we had the back-up footage on tape. This eliminates the digitizing process and shaves time off our editing. (See **Figure 6.4.**)

Figure 6.4 Our camera attached to the Sony laptop with DV Rack HD.

However, because we were shooting for air immediately, HDV footage (MPEG-2) would not be our choice in editing. We needed to downconvert the footage to standard definition for this project—but this will be explained shortly.

What a Pro!

Adobe Premiere Pro 2 was selected for editing because we were familiar with Adobe's earlier (non-HDV) versions of Premiere. As mentioned earlier, we shot our footage in 1080i, CineFrame 24 with the Sony Z1. As of this writing, many local television stations cannot air footage in 1080i (at least they could not locally on the three channels chosen by the advertising agency to air this spot). Therefore, the end product had to be standard definition. However, these "commercials" had three other uses:

1. The two attorneys wanted to constantly update the clients used in the testimonials so viewers would not be seeing the same group of people over and over. They wanted 10 different commercials with five possible endings. This is called a *donut*, because the middle (the hole) stays the same (how can you change a hole?) and the rest of the spot changes. As the law firm contracted with other people to use in the testimonials, we would use one of the five possible attorney-speaking middles, with new testimonial people. Nonlinear editing shines here because we would simply make minor changes to the file when new people were added. When HDV becomes the norm, stations will want commercials in high definition, and our attorneys wanted to jump on this bandwagon.

2. Our clients also wanted these spots to appear on the Web. Of course the bandwidth of an HDV commercial is far too large to upload or download on the Internet. Again, a low-resolution, standard definition version would need to be edited that would reside on the attorneys' Web site.

3.   Lastly, our clients wanted DVDs of these commercials to show to prospective new clients. These versions also needed to be in standard definition because few homeowners were HDV capable in their abodes at the time. We would always have the HDV footage that could be mastered in HDV when the time was right—but for now we had to stick to all standard definition versions.

Our decision in editing was not a difficult one, especially with the Sony Z1. Since we knew the end product had to be in standard definition for airing on television, we had the Sony automatically downconvert the files to letterbox NTSC, giving us the black bands at the top and bottom of the screen.

Because we used DV Rack HD, we had our footage already downconverted on our Maxtor hard drive. Using Adobe's Premiere Pro 2 would make our edit process fast and smooth. (See **Figure 6.5**.)

Figure 6.5 Adobe Premiere Pro 2 on our Sony Vaio laptop.

Once Adobe Premiere Pro 2 has been opened, and New Project is selected, you are taken to a screen that asks a few questions. Here is where you can select your "presets" with the following options: Adobe HD-SDI, which includes 1080i 25, 1080i 30, 1080p 24, 720p 60; Adobe HDV with HDV 1080i 25 (Sony 50), HDV 1080i 30 (Sony 60), our choice if we were editing in native HDV, or HDV 720p 30 if using the JVC HD100U; Adobe SD-SDI which includes NTSC and PAL; DV-24p, which incorporates standard 32kHz, standard 48kHz, Widescreen 32kHz, and Widescreen 48kHz; DV-NTSC which has the same options as DV-24p, except you are now posting in 24 frames; and finally DV-PAL, which also has the same kilohertz options only in PAL.

The description will appear on the right after you have made your selection. We chose the SD-SDI NTSC option because the footage was already standard definition when downconverted and saved to DV Rack HD, we did not shoot in 24 frames progressive although we did shoot in 24-frame mode, and our footage was letterbox so widescreen would not have been an acceptable choice (only for viewing on 16:9 monitors).

Selecting this option gave us the following in the description field, "for editing uncompressed SD, interlaced 10-bit (4:2:2) SD video at 29.97 frames per second, 48kHz audio, drop frame timecode numbering." The frame size would be 720 × 480 letterbox, with the lower field first option selected.

Premiere then opens with your project. The layout of the software is much like the competition so it is not worth addressing here. The program and source monitors open with 4:3 aspect ratio windows because the downconverted footage is letterbox and not widescreen. We still need to edit and keep everything in standard definition.

NOTE: As a reminder, letterbox is viewed in the 4:3 aspect ratio with the black bands on the top and bottom of the screen; widescreen is a 16:9 aspect ratio with the image filling the entire frame with no black bars. If widescreen is viewed on a 4:3 screen, the footage is squeezed because it is trying to fit 16:9 material in 4:3 space.

The first five commercials were posted this way and exported to DVD (more on this later). The television networks airing the spots still require all footage to be submitted on Betacam SP because MiniDV is not yet an acceptable format for broadcast.

After 2007, when our local stations will be airing high definition, the footage on the MiniDV tapes will be digitized for the first time (remember, we downconverted it into Serious Magic's DV Rack HD, and now we need the native footage because we will output in HDV). At this point we will select Adobe HDV and HDV 1080i 30 (Sony 60), which gives us access via FireWire to the Sony Z1 with 16:9 interlaced HD video at 29.97 fps. The frame size will be 1440 × 1080 (1.333) with the upper field first.

The source and program monitors become 16:9 and Capture is selected from the File menu. The footage will be converted to MPEG-2 files for the editing process—and the rest is history.

This project was unique in that we edited the downconverted footage in standard definition letterbox because we needed versions that would air on television and low resolution versions for the Web. When HDV versions are needed a short time later, it makes more sense to digitize the original footage again rather than upconverting the downconverted footage (too much compression). The original material will be sharper because it was shot in HDV and it will also air that way.

Project Two: The Backyard

Our second scenario uses Ulead's Media Studio Pro 8 NLE software, which includes Video Capture and Video Editor. The footage this time was shot with the JVC HD100U in 720p/30, and the project was a 20-minute documentary on how many eco-systems are found in the average neighborhood backyard. Each of the creatures that reside there had to be videotaped day and night (some were nocturnal) for an HD program for a local PBS-member station.

Our director of photography had a 10:1 ratio—200 minutes of tape for a 20-minute program. The animals usually did not cooperate while on camera. Of course, as soon as we were in the middle of changing tapes, they performed perfectly. (The old warning against working with children and animals is so very, very true.) With four tapes filled with footage, we had a lot of capturing to do.

Normally we would have used DV Rack because it would have saved all of the capturing time, but we were on location in the woods and did not have enough battery power for continuous power for the computer and external hard drive. We had to use the old-fashioned routine of playing back the recorded footage onto the computer.

For post, we used Media Studio Pro 8 because it makes fast work of the capturing process and it is a user-friendly edit system. You can edit the file in either MPEG format files or Microsoft AVI files. Because we would be editing native HDV, we selected MPEG. If the finished product was going to be SD, only a PC's AVI file would suffice—Apple's QuickTime is not supported. Like Premiere Pro, you have additional choices once you decide to MPEG or not to MPEG. When you make your selection, the Properties box displays the corresponding information. In our case,

HDV 720/30p is displayed: NTSC drop frame, 29.97 fps, MPEG file, 24 bits, 1280 × 720 16:9 MPEG-2 with a video data rate of 18300 kbps and an audio data rate of 384 kbps.

When you open the video capture window, you again must make several choices. You can auto capture if you have your shots already logged or use manual mode. You can capture at a specific frame rate, auto name the file, and capture audio. You may also cut when a file reaches a certain size (never a good idea in our opinion), and cut when a new scene is detected. We selected everything in the manual mode.

Choose your capture device (the name of the camera) and the capture format (MPEG, in our case). Once you click on the record button, the NLE begins capturing the footage. Because conversion to MPEG-2 is part of the process, you will see the footage as it happens live on the screen, but the conversion process takes a little time. A 25-second shot of a squirrel may take over a minute to convert after you stop ingesting the footage. This is a necessary evil of native HDV editing when you are converting to an elementary stream (because the camera is supposedly shooting in MPEG-2), a limitation on processing speed that will hopefully be eliminated as computers become faster. See **Figures 6.6** and **6.7**.

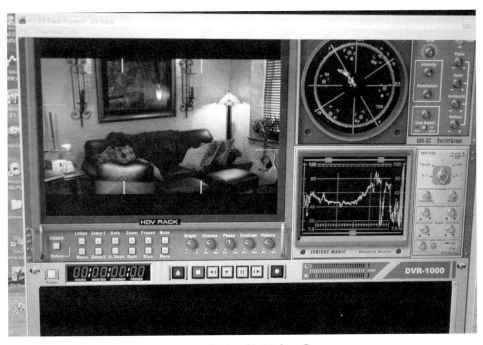

Figure 6.6 A view of Ulead's Video Capture screen.

Figure 6.7 A view of the Ulead's Video Editor user interface.

When you are capturing or digitizing footage, allow the computer enough time to store or build the shot before you begin ingesting the next one. Your system will likely crash if you try to do too much too quickly. This is your first exercise in patience, but remember that HDV files are larger than SD files.

Footage is taken into the source window (16:9) and the in and out points marked. This is just our way of selecting the footage. You can take the footage directly to the timeline and edit there, but that's not our workflow. Either way, editing from this point on follows the same rules as SD. (A jump cut in HD is just as unacceptable as a jump cut in SD.) We dropped our shots of the squirrel, hummingbird, opossum, and other natives into the timeline and created a clean 20-minute program.

When your editing is complete, select Export and choose whether you want DVD Authoring or DV Recording. You may also select Playback Options, where the quality can be set somewhere between low and high. If you choose DVD Authoring, DVD Movie Factory opens and allows you to add media to the DVD, create a menu, and add or edit chapters. On a 4.7-gigabyte DVD, you are also given a running total on how much space has been used. These are still large files, which is why having enough RAM on your computer is imperative. Without this buffer, a computer may declare "insufficient disk space" and freeze.

This is not real-time editing because of the lag time with the MPEG-2 conversion. But once the conversion is complete, you can edit as usual.

Project Three: Chasing Waterfalls

Our third scenario involves using Sony Vegas 6.0 as our NLE system incorporating footage we shot with the Canon XL H1. The waterfall footage mentioned in Chapter 4 was to be used as a promotional piece for a local chamber of commerce. The chamber had large 16:9 monitors in their information area, and tourists could wander in and watch a loop of this waterfall footage.

Shooting in 1080i/60, we wanted the smoothest possible flow of the water in order to tell our story visually. Having tested the camera in its 30-frame and 24-frame modes, we thought the water looked too pixelly in those formats. The 60-frame mode gave the water a more blurry, slow-shutter-speed look, much as if you had taken a still photograph with a three-second exposure to blur the appearance of the water. See **Figure 6.8**.

Figure 6.8 The blurred look of the waterfall was the look we were after, so we shot in 1080i/60.

One 60-minute MiniDV tape and we had more than enough footage for the five-minute video that would be looped on a DVD. Because we were stationed only a few feet from millions of gallons of water, we did not use DV Rack for fear of insufficient power or an unfortunate meeting between the laptop and the rocks at the bottom of the waterfall. (Any more of these nature shoots and maybe it'll be time to invest in a portable hard disk re-corder such as the one from FOCUS Enhancements that we borrowed for review in Chapter 4.) As a result, all footage needed to be digitized and incorporated into our NLE program.

Using the Canon XL H1 as the transfer tool, Sony Vegas was powered up on our Sony Vaio, Pentium 4 desktop. As illustrated in **Figure 6.9,** the user interface of the Vegas looks different from any other NLE we have used. For example, the Preview Monitor appears at the bottom of the screen rather than at the top as with other NLE systems. You can extend it to any size, but it is still going to live on the bottom. Also, the audio monitor LEDs are on the left of the screen while the timeline is on top. If you have used other NLE systems, it will take some getting used to, but once you are familiar with the unique layout, it is a great program for post.

Figure 6.9 The Sony Vegas editing screen looks different from other NLE systems. (Photo courtesy of Sony)

Under the File menu, Capture Video is selected and a full-screen monitor appears. This is a smart feature; when you are capturing or digitizing, it is your main focus and it should fill the screen. With the other NLE programs you can make the capture video as large as you like, but Sony does not give you an option—it just fills the screen. You have three menu icons at the top of the screen: Capture, Advanced Capture, and Print to Tape. In the Capture mode, you can capture video, audio, the entire tape, or an image. With the usual transport feature, the buttons all become highlighted once the camera is connected. With a menu accessible at all times, if you run into a problem or cannot find where Vegas is hiding an icon, help is always there to walk you through the process.

Select the Options menu and open Preferences. Six tabs (general, disk management, capture, advanced capture, print to tape, and preview) let you set all of your parameters. Under the general tab alone, you have 15 choices to check or uncheck. Disk management allows you to view how much space you have available for editing on your hard drive(s). Capture asks more questions as well as allows custom frame rates. It is a good idea to walk through all of these before you select your choices.

Vegas was one of the first NLE choices that allowed HDV support and provided automatic setup, depending on the camera. When the camera is attached and recognized, you cannot select your options so you do not have any choices here. The icons are large and easy to view on the timeline, and the video and audio scrubbing feature is the best we have seen on an NLE. Our project was output at 1440 × 1080 at 29.97 fps interlaced.

We have discussed three separate projects on three different NLE systems using different HDV camcorders. We have not detailed Avid or Apple, two of the other major players in the NLE realm, but they are similar to the NLE systems we covered and should offer similar workflow possibilities if one of them is your system of choice.

Despite the claims of marketing hype, no one NLE system is the "end all" in the world of post production. Every editor has a favorite NLE system—or at least one on which they feel the most comfortable. Hopefully, the three we have discussed give you a good feel for the workflow. Again, HDV is not that much different from SD in the sense that good visual and audio aesthetics still apply, as do good editing techniques. As always, your creativity combined with good technical technique will fuel the success of your project.

This brings up another term you should be aware of—intermediate codecs (short for coder/decoders). Software programs such as Canopus and CineForm have codecs that decrease the loss in post production and run much faster on a computer than MPEG will through the editing process. "It's all in the codec" still applies. Without the proper codec (a necessary tool in editing), your end result will suffer.

Points of Interest

- Various NLE systems provide a way to ingest digital video for editing.

- Be familiar with the capture options available in the NLE system you use.

- Due to limitations in processing power, your NLE system may not be able to capture HDV footage in real time.

Being Content with Content Delivery

Once you have shot your footage, ingested it into your NLE, and edited your final project, it is time to address content delivery. Unless you invite the masses over to your place to review the results or take your hard drive on a road trip, you must export your project to a medium that others can access and view. The three choices for sharing the fruit of your labors are videotape, DVD, or the World Wide Web, though there are, of course, options within these options.

Our discussion begins with videotape. If your HDV footage has been edited natively in HDV and you will be outputting that in the same format (either 1080i or 720p), the ideal videotape choice is MiniDV. Of course, your footage may only be played back on an HDV VTR, but you have lost no image quality, your project has not been subjected to additional compression (unless you are editing extremely long material with numerous digital effects will require recompression for output), and it is still in the digital realm. Unfortunately, this is not the most realistic option for mass consumption. Most homeowners, clients, or other recipients do not have access to HDV decks, so unless you're willing to invest in some serious hardware on behalf of others, you will have to make some compromises.

Perhaps the most accessible option in videotape is VHS. The Video Home System (VHS originally stood for the Vertical Helical Scan technology it uses), introduced in the United States in 1977, has a resolution of 240 horizontal lines in NTSC. That is a far cry from the 720 or 1080 lines of resolution that are a part of the HDV specification. You can output your project to VHS, but you will run into problems, starting with the image itself. While VHS is certainly watchable—a videotape format doesn't last for 30 years by accident—it is simply not capable of showing the resolution of your original material.

If the end user will be watching your VHS copy in their homes, will they have their VHS deck hooked up to a 16:9 monitor? It is possible that some might, but VHS will not look very good if the monitor is set up to stretch the 4:3 VHS image. If your end product is letterboxed or edge cropped to fit a 4:3 set, it still won't have the HD resolution of your original, but it will look better than a stretched-out version of your downconverted SD content. Either way, even for a rough cut review, the resolution limitations of VHS make it a poor choice for showcasing HD material.

Another tape-based option is S-VHS or Super VHS. Introduced in 1987, this format has 430 lines of horizontal resolution, making it far superior to VHS. It is still an analog alternative, however, and S-VHS never achieved the popularity of VHS. Still, you can purchase S-VHS decks, sometimes in combo units with other formats. Once you have a deck in place, how do you get the best signal to your monitor? It helps to have connections.

D-VHS

Originally, Digital VHS (D-VHS) was supposed to be a new consumer format, a digital replacement of the king of consumer video, VHS. Of course, upgrading VHS had been tried before. S-VHS had made the attempt with promises of better pictures and consumers barely noticed (though it did carve out a small niche for itself in educational settings and small-market ENG applications). This time, D-VHS offered digital recording and high definition, plus it maintained backward compatibility to libraries of VHS tapes so they would not become obsolete.

The D-VHS system recorded the MPEG-2 bit stream itself and then decoded it for playback. That meant it could record HD programs and even multicasting content. In addition, selectable data rates allowed users to record up to 49 hours of content at the lowest quality or more than three hours of HD at the highest quality on a single cassette.

JVC introduced the HM-DSR1000 digital satellite recorder in 1997, and once again, consumers shrugged their collective shoulders. Part of the problem was its reliance on satellite TV service; you couldn't record an MPEG-2 signal from cable. The major problem, however, was price. The D-VHS unit sold with a satellite dish for about $1,000 (or without the dish for the bargain price of $950). Considering a serious lack of HD programming available at the time, D-VHS couldn't offer much return for such a major investment. (See **Figure 6.10**.)

Figure 6.10 D-VHS began as a consumer format but has found its niche with professional applications. (Photo courtesy of JVC)

But a funny thing happened on the way to obscurity; D-VHS experienced a renaissance on the professional level. D-VHS had originally been engineered with a FireWire port. As a result, it could be connected to HDV camcorders and record (and then play-back) the bit stream in full HD quality. In addition, JVC introduced a ProHD D-VHS player and record deck, which were different from the consumer model in that they offered password protection of content. Now, Hollywood producers could watch high-quality digital dailies of the day's shoot securely—and without the expense of a projectionist, film projector, and processing multiple prints of the film footage.

It's All in the Wires

The output to a television from a standard VHS player may be relayed to the monitor in one of two ways. The first is through a *radio frequency* (RF) coaxial cable that carries the video and audio signals from the output of the VCR to the input of the television. Designed to carry a maximum of 525 lines in the United States (and 625 lines in PAL countries), coax has been a cornerstone of the cable TV and satellite industries for content delivery to the home. Of course, VHS only offers 240 lines of resolution, so coax is more than sufficient to support a VHS signal from a VCR to a monitor.

The better option is to split the video and audio signal into separate cables, which provides a better picture. This is when you use the RCA or BNC video out on your VHS deck (usually color-coded yellow) to the video in on your TV (also yellow). The audio is usually split into a stereo left and right (white and red) RCA connection. This gives you a slightly better picture because the video and audio are not combined in a single cable. Again, this is adequate for SD signals.

When S-VHS came along, viewers wanted to see these extra horizontal lines of resolution and a new method of connection was needed, the *S-Video* cable. If you split the RF coaxial cable that carries both video and audio into a cable that carries just the video and the other just the audio, how much better performance could you get if you split the video signal into two separate signals? That's exactly what the S-Video cable does—it carries just the video signal but splits it into a chrominance (color) and luminance (brightness) signal.

The S-Video cable sports a gold connection on each end with several pins. The brightness and color are now separate signals, so clarity is increased.

This is the best way to view S-VHS footage and is even acceptable for some DVD material. Audio has nothing at all to do with this cable, however, and must be connected separately, often through the RCA connections on the deck.

But there is still room for improvement. If manufacturers could split the chrominance and luminance in an S-Video cable into two signals, how much better would it be if it were split into three different signals? Thus the *component* signal was implemented. The video is divided between three color-coded cables—red, green, and blue—that allow the sharpest image possible.

The human eye only sees in red, green, and blue; any other "color" you might see is your brain mixing these three color signals. The video industry came out with the RGB connection that allowed computer monitors and high-end graphic users to split the signal into these three primary colors. By varying the intensity of the red, green, and blue signal, every color in the visible spectrum can be seen.

The problem with an RGB (and component video) connection is that it gobbles up bandwidth, and that is not cheap. The first part of this signal is the luminance signal. This is called the "Y" component. The other two signals are called "color difference," which indicate how much blue and red there is relative to luminance. Each of these is given a name and you probably have seen these on the back of your DVD player or recorder— "B-Y" for the blue component and "R-Y" for the red. Basically, these are mathematical derivatives of the older RGB signal. This is really an improvement of the old color-under-video system. The cable used for this connection usually has color-coded RCA ends that fit into the corresponding color inputs or outputs.

By not using an RGB cable, we can reduce the bandwidth by a third. But broadcasters still need even more compression. You may be wondering what happened to the green color signal? It does not need to be transmitted as a separate signal because it is pulled from the Y, B-Y, and R-Y combination.

This is where PAL and NTSC came into play with composite video. Picture information is lost when component video is compressed and aired as a composite signal, and if you compress luminance and chrominance into one signal, you can never "unseparate" them again. This appears on the screen as a degraded image.

DVDs are encoded with this component signal. The connection on your DVD unit may display Y, B-Y, and R-Y, but it may also be Y, Pb, Pr, or Y, Cb, Cr.

The DVD Option

Why deliver on DVD? According to the Consumer Electronics Association, there are more than 147 million component DVD players in the United States, and portable DVD players and DVD recorders are among the fastest-growing consumer electronics product groups. This also appears to be the method of choice for content delivery. A single-sided DVD allows 4.7 gigabytes of information. This is called a *DVD-5* because it holds almost five gigabytes of information. Depending on the *bit rate* (remember that term), you may fit up to 60 minutes of high-quality video on one side of the disk. Dual layer or two-sided discs will accept up to 9.4 gigabytes of information. This is called a *DVD-9*.

With DVD recording technology, your project can be viewed on DVD and given to almost anyone. The discs are very inexpensive and reasonably rugged (when stored properly in a case), and they provide a semipermanent method for showing your work to the world . . . with a few exceptions.

The world has different "zones" or "regions" where DVDs can be viewed. The United States uses Zone 1, the United Kingdom uses Zone 2, and so on. If the DVD is coded for Zone 2, for example, it will not play in the United States.

But when recording or burning your DVDs, you can select the zone or zones in which they can be played. Depending on what authoring software you use, "zone free" DVDs can also be made that will play anywhere in the world.

There also are rewriteable options out there. With DVD–RW and DVD+RW, you can read and rewrite up to 1,000 times. This is by far the easiest mode: play back the footage to the client, make any changes necessary, erase the disc and reburn it.

But the problem with this technology is that only one hour of standard definition footage will reside on a DVD-R at the highest quality bit rate. You can easily put more information on the disc, but the quality goes down with more information. When renting or purchasing a feature film on DVD, the quality looks outstanding (for standard definition). That is because most feature films are shot on 35mm motion-picture film, which has 5,000 plus lines of horizontal resolution—far superior to any HDV format. If you shoot something in this mode and put it on a lesser medium like DVD, it is still going to look phenomenal.

The bit rate can be changed in some DVD authoring programs so more information can fit on a standard 4.7-gigabyte DVD. Like recording at LP (long play) speed on your MiniDV player, you are recording at a lesser bit rate. The lower the bit rate, the more footage you can squeeze onto a DVD, but there will be a noticeable difference in picture quality.

A common misconception is that HDV footage takes up more space on a DVD than SD material. When editing, 1080i or 720p uses more memory when converting the image to MPEG-2, but it uses the same compression rate (25 Mbps) as standard definition MiniDV. However, if the footage is true high definition, it will take up more space. That means you can edit to your heart's content and still fit that 25-minute epic on one DVD. We are basically creating a standard definition DVD and that is why it is manageable. Just remember that DVD only provides 480 lines of resolution, so your audience will be viewing a 480p version of your HDV project.

Out of the Blue (Laser)

As mentioned briefly in Chapter 2, manufacturers have introduced competing high definition DVD formats, which could eventually become another distribution medium for your HDV project. One of the technologies is Blu-ray disc (BD). Plans for the format were announced in 2002, and format specifications were completed in early 2006. It was developed by the Blu-ray Disc Association (BDA), which counts a number of industry leaders as members, including JVC, Panasonic, Samsung, Sharp, Sony, Thomson, and more. The technology was developed so you could store large amounts of data (including HD video) on a recordable and rewriteable disc. A single layer Blu-ray DVD can hold up to 25 GB of data per side (50 GB for a dual-layer disc), more than five times the capacity of DVD.

With DVD recordable media, a red laser is used to read and write the disc. Blu-ray uses a blue-violet laser to handle the same task. The wavelength of the violet laser is shorter (405 nm) than the red laser (650 nm), which allows the laser to focus more precisely and store more data in less space. All of the major studios except one (we won't tell) have agreed to release titles in Blu-ray and DVD. Most Blu-ray players will be backward compatible with existing DVDs, so your current collection will not become obsolete. Expect to see a recordable disc for HD movies and computer data (BD-R), a re-writable version (BD-RE), and a read-only format for the distribution of movies, software, and games (BD-ROM).

High-definition digital video disc, or HD-DVD, is the other emerging optical disc format. This one is backed by the DVD Forum (originally named the DVD Consortium), which defined the original DVD format specifications in the 1990s. The same size as the Blu-ray solution (120mm) and using the same type of violet-blue laser, Toshiba, Sanyo, Microsoft, and NEC are backing this format. With a smaller 15 GB capacity per side (30 for a dual layer), Toshiba says it is developing a three-layer disc to raise capacity to 45 GB per side.

Table 6.1 illustrates the similarities and differences between DVD and the two formats hoping to replace it in the marketplace. In the last box under video codecs, we included the terms MPEG-4 and SMPTE VC-1. MPEG-4 is the newest generation MPEG variant, while VC-1 is Windows Media's newest contender.

Table 6.1 Comparison of DVD, Blu-ray, and HD-DVD Formats. (Courtesy of *www.blu-ray.com*)

Parameters	DVD	Blu-ray	HD-DVD
Storage Capacity	4.7 GB (single layer) 8.5 GB (dual layer)	25 GB (single layer) 50 GB (dual layer)	15 GB (single layer) 30 GB (dual layer)
Laser Wavelength	650 nm (red laser)	405 nm (blue laser)	405 nm (blue laser)
Numerical Aperture	0.60	0.85	0.65
Disc Diameter	120 mm	120 mm	120 mm
Disc Thickness	1.2 mm	1.2 mm	1.2 mm
Protection Layer	0.6 mm	0.1 mm	0.6 mm
Hard Coating	No	Yes	No
Track Pitch	0.74 μm	0.32 μm	0.40 μm
Data Transfer Rate (data and video)	11.08 Mbps	36.0 Mbps (1×) 54.0 Mbps (1.5×)	36.55 Mbps (1×)
Video Bit Rate	9.8 Mbps	1080p 40.0 Mbps	1080p 28.0 Mbps
Video Resolution	720 × 480 (480i)	1920 × 1080	1920 × 1080
Video Codecs	MPEG-2	MPEG-2, MPEG-4 AVC, SMPTE VC-1	MPEG-2, MPEG-4, AVC, SMPTE VC-1

Send in the Clones

There are two words you will need to know in making multiple copies of your DVD—duplication and replication. Duplication is where you (or someone else) makes clones (copies) of your master DVD onto recordable media (DVD-R, DVD+R). When you copy one analog tape to another, you lose information. This is called a generation loss, and while it might not be terribly noticeable on the first copy, generation loss adds up to poor pictures quickly. A digital copy is an exact duplicate, with no generation loss, which is why it is called a clone and not a copy.

The problem with duplication of DVD-R technology is that, while many DVD players will play them, not every player will accept a DVD-R or DVD+R disc. With dozens of manufacturers making recordable media and the same number making their own DVD recorders, the tolerances are just too wide. The best option is replication.

Replication is where you have a company create copies of your DVD from a stamped master rather than recordable media. This process involves having the firm make a glass master of your disc in a dust-free environment and stamp numerous clones from molten plastic that will play in 100 percent of the DVD players out there (assuming the proper regional coding, of course).

So why doesn't everyone have their discs replicated rather than duplicated? The main factor is cost. Hiring a facility to create a glass master in a dust-free environment comes with a hefty price tag. Major motion picture studios that sell thousands or millions of copies can afford the expense, but it might not be in the budget for the independent filmmakers. Plus, do you really need replication if you are only going to produce a few dozen copies?

The last problem with DVDs is labeling. You can label a recordable DVD cheaply by writing on the nonrecorded side with a Sharpie or other permanent marker. That is fine for internal use, but not always professional enough for your clients. The better option is to purchase DVDs with printable labels (inkjet, thermal, or laser).

Several manufacturers such as Primera and Rimage offer DVD/CD duplicators that will burn and label up to 50 blank discs at a time. These discs may be either +R or –R, and Primera has created a Blu-ray DVD duplicator that will make digital copies of these discs as well. If you need a few copies or even hundreds, it is usually less expensive to duplicate the discs than to incur the cost of replication.

Points of Interest

- Established analog consumer tape standards such as VHS are a poor choice for delivering HDV content.

- New blue-laser DVD formats promise increased capacity and HD playback.

- Replication uses a glass master in a dust-free environment, while duplication is done using DVD-R technology.

CHAPTER 7

Beyond HDV

Since its introduction in 2003, the HDV format has continued to gain momentum in the video industry at every level. For consumers, it provides a medium that captures high definition recordings of dance recitals and birthday parties without refinancing the family home. For nonbroadcast video professionals, it makes available the strategic business benefit and creative freedom of HD without the traditionally cost-prohibitive price tag. And for broadcasters, it offers the competitive advantage of HD production for local news and programming at a more reasonable price than other HD options.

But it's not alone. A handful of manufacturers have already begun to test the low-end HD market with their non-HDV solutions, and more are sure to follow. Grass Valley, a Thomson brand, has introduced the company's first camcorder, Infinity, which offers HD acquisition using off-the-shelf Iomega® REV® removable hard disk and CompactFlash® recording media. Panasonic has expanded its DVCPRO HD camcorder line to include a substantially lower-priced unit that uses the company's proprietary solid-state recording media. Even Sony, one of the industry's leading HDV supporters, has introduced an optical disc system that provides HD options beyond the HDV format. And Ikegami, which pioneered tapeless acquisition, offers an HD camcorder as well.

While this book is focused on HDV, it would be remiss to ignore competing HD acquisition technologies that are at or near the price range of current HDV products. While the camcorder offerings from Grass Valley, Sony, and Ikegami are more than $10,000, they are still a fraction of the cost of high-end HD camcorders. The following pages outline competing formats and products, with a special emphasis on the technologies and workflows that might make them an attractive alternative to HDV.

Panasonic DVCPRO HD

DVCPRO HD is the third in a series of DV-based digital video formats from Panasonic. As the industry began to offer digital alternatives to the Sony Betacam SP analog workhorse, Panasonic delivered DVCPRO in 1995, its proprietary 4:1:1, 25 Mbps DV format meant to compete directly with Sony's DVCAM family of products. DVCPRO50 soon followed, a 4:2:2, 50 Mbps version of the format that provided better images through increased bit rates and less compression. And then came DVCPRO HD, a 100 Mbps format that provided high definition images in 720p or 1080i. DVCPRO HD camcorders began shipping in 2000, two years after the first Sony HDCAM camcorders were available.

The Varicam (AJ-HDC27) camcorder is the pinnacle of the DVCPRO HD line, a popular choice for episodic television, commercials, and documentaries. Like the Sony HDW-900H HDCAM alternative, however, it costs close to $100,000 by the time you have it outfitted with a lens and accessories. While these cameras deliver amazing quality, they are clearly not designed to appeal to the low-cost HD market.

After it helped develop the HDV standard in 2003, Sony introduced its first professional HDV camcorder, the HVR-Z1U, in 2004. Eager to get a piece of the low-cost HD action—without hopping on the Sony-backed HDV format bandwagon—Panasonic unveiled its own solution in 2005, the AG-HVX200, which brought the DVCPRO HD format to the low-cost marketplace when units began shipping in late 2005. (The camcorder's list price was just under $6,000 when it was first available.) The even bigger news was that the camcorder recorded on the company's proprietary P2 solid-state memory cards, which the company introduced in 2003 and delivered to customers the following year.

Solid-State Memory

While other manufacturers were focused on hard disk and optical disc recording solutions, Panasonic leapfrogged the competition with its P2 introduction in 2003. P2 uses solid-state technology to record audio and video footage, the same technology used in today's digital still cameras. Comparatively, though, professional video is a memory hog. While a 1 GB CompactFlash card holds hundreds or thousands of still images (depending on your camera's settings), an 8 GB P2 card (shown in **Figure 7.1**) only holds about 32 minutes of DV footage or eight minutes of DVCPRO HD (though you can store more footage shooting in 24p because you are recording fewer frames per second).

Figure 7.1 Panasonic's P2 proprietary solid-state recording media is used in a number of the company's camcorders. (Photo courtesy of Panasonic)

Despite its memory-hungry nature, solid-state has several advantages over tape-based media. Nonlinear editing systems can access solid-state drives directly, so there's no time-consuming ingest required (assuming you are not converting your files, of course). Solid-state also has no moving parts, which makes it more reliable in principle than tape, optical disc, or even hard disk, which all rely on mechanical movement during recording. Panasonic's P2 camcorders also feature multiple P2 card slots that are hot-swappable, and its solid-state media supports thousands of rewrite cycles without quality loss. P2 cards have a PCMCIA CardBus form factor, so they can be used with laptop computers. Meanwhile, Grass Valley has taken a nonproprietary approach to solid-state media—its Infinity camcorder is designed to use CompactFlash cards, which are widely available and manufactured by a number of companies.

Some experts have said solid-state is an idea ahead of its time for the broadcast industry, due to the cost-prohibitive nature of memory. However, as memory capacity continues to increase and prices continue to decrease, solid-state recording has the potential to be the preferred acquisition technology of the future.

When you think about it, the move made perfect sense. Panasonic was already satisfied with its DVCPRO HD format; it was well established in the industry and already supported by several major editing platforms. The new camcorder not only incorporated a familiar codec but introduced P2 to a potentially much wider audience (previously it had only been available in DVCPRO and DVCPRO50 ENG-style camcorders that cost more than $10,000).

As shown in **Figure 7.2**, the HVX200 camcorder itself resembles an over-stuffed AG-DVX100, one of Panasonic's most popular MiniDV professional camcorders. It features three, 1/3-inch CCDs (native 16:9), 14-bit digital signal processing, and 16-bit, four-channel audio. Its built-in 13× Leica zoom lens offers optical image stabilization and focus assist.

Figure 7.2 The Panasonic AG-HVX200 acquires footage using the DVCPRO HD format, which supports 720p and 1080i HD acquisition with a variety of frame rates. (Photo courtesy of Panasonic)

For editing, the DVCPRO HD codec has an advantage over HDV in that each frame of video is independent; no interframe compression here. Instead, DVCPRO HD uses intraframe compression, much like that used in DV. The HVX200 is compatible with a number of NLE systems, including Apple Final Cut Pro (though it does need to transcode the file), Canopus EDIUS HD, and several Avid solutions. DVFilm's Raylight software transcodes the DVCPRO HD files to AVI files, so footage can be edited by other NLEs, including Adobe Premiere Pro and Sony Vegas.

The DVCPRO HD format supports recording in 1080i/60, 1080p/24, 1080p/30, and 720p with variable frame rates (including 24, 30, and 60 fps). In addition, the HVX200 records in DVCPRO 50, DVCPRO, and DV. The camcorder also records to MiniDV tape, but only in the 25 Mbps DV mode. However, you can shoot in HD, record to P2 cards, and then down-convert to SD to MiniDV tape using internal processing. There is also a FireStore FS-100 hard disk recording solution from FOCUS Enhancements, which can store close to 100 minutes of 720p or 1080i content.

As shown in **Table 7.1**, DVCPRO HD compression has a number of advantages over HDV. It not only uses less compression, but its intraframe compression scheme is more amenable to nonlinear editing, and it has more frequent sampling of chrominance. However, the DVCPRO HD format actually has less horizontal resolution than HDV, and its bit rate is too large to be recorded onto MiniDV tape.

Table 7.1 Comparison of DVCPRO HD and HDV format specifications.

	Bit Rate	Compression Type	Sampling Frequency	Progressive Resolution	Interlaced Resolution
DVCPRO HD	100 Mbps	Intraframe	4:2:2	960 × 720	1280 × 1080
HDV	19 or 25 Mbps	Interframe	4:2:0	1280 × 720	1440 × 1080

While DVCPRO HD has a higher bit rate, HDV offers more horizontal pixels. (Note, interlaced resolution of DVCPRO HD improves to 1440 × 1080 when shooting at 25 fps.)

DVCPRO HD footage takes a lot of storage (one minute of HD footage requires roughly 1 GB, though 24p footage uses less storage because fewer frames are recorded), and P2 cards are too expensive to use like videotape, where you save your raw footage tapes and only recycle them (if ever) when your project is complete. If you are going to work with P2, you are going to have to develop a different workflow. For one thing, you need to figure out where you are going to store your raw footage and how you are going to get it there.

For the field, Panasonic offers the AJ-PCS060 DVCPRO P2 Store, a ruggedized 60 GB hard drive. You can transfer your footage into the drive at the rate of about 1 GB per minute, then refill your P2 cards with new footage. The P2 Store may be seen by an NLE as an external hard drive via USB 2.0. Once you are back in your post suite, you can import footage from the HVX200 into your NLE via FireWire, or you can install a P2 Drive (AJ-PCD10) into your PC.

Points of Interest

- The AG-HVX200 offers a true low-cost HD acquisition alternative to HDV.

- Panasonic's proprietary P2 solid-state memory card format requires a new workflow.

- The DVCPRO HD format produces much larger video files than HDV, so more storage will be required.

Grass Valley Infinity

The Infinity Digital Media Camcorder was the first camcorder released by Grass Valley, a company that is known more for its production switchers and servers. It is part of a series of Infinity products designed to utilize off-the-shelf media, as opposed to video industry-specific recording media. "Our goal is nothing less than the death of proprietary recording media," declared Jeff Rosica, Grass Valley vice president of marketing and business development, during an interview for *Television Broadcast* magazine in 2005. "We believe that our open format approach will also put an end to manufacturers dictating future format purchasing decisions for their customers and limiting the kind of recording choices that users have."

While the HDV standard was designed to record on MiniDV videotape, the Infinity series of products is based around a choice of Iomega REV and REV PRO removable disks and CompactFlash solid-state memory for acquisition. Granted, REV PRO was created by Iomega specifically for Infinity, and consumer-grade CompactFlash cards will not hold a particularly large amount of HD footage, but there is something to be said for running into a local office supply or neighborhood electronics superstore

Figure 7.3 The Infinity Digital Media camcorder offers a variety of recording media choices as well as recording formats. (Photo courtesy of Grass Valley)

when you are in a pinch for recording media. It was one of the early selling points of HDV, and it is an advantage shared by Infinity.

The Infinity camcorder prototype was unveiled in 2005, and the camcorder began shipping in 2006. It records in a variety of formats: 525i/60 and 625i/50 for SD, as well as 720p/50, 720p/60, 1080i/50, and 1080i/60 for HD. It features three, 2/3-inch CCDs and 14-bit processing. There are two slots for CompactFlash cards. However, its use of solid-state memory is plagued by the same problems as Panasonic's P2: high bit rates, limited storage capacity. One 8 GB CompactFlash card holds about 10 minutes of 75 Mbps HD or 15 minutes of 50 Mbps HD. The 35 GB REV PRO hard disk cartridge offers increased capacity—up to 45 or 65 minutes of HD, again based on bit rate. The REV PRO cartridge is a more robust version of Iomega's standard REV drive, providing a higher data rate than the consumer version and dual data stream capability (you can record and transfer files simultaneously), which is not supported by standard REV.

Infinity's compression of choice is JPEG 2000. Developed by the Joint Photographic Experts Group (JPEG), JPEG 2000 uses a wavelet transform algorithm across the entire image. As a result, wavelet artifacts look more like image blur, a more visually appealing prospect than the more noticeable macroblocks in other digital systems.

Another advantage to JPEG 2000 compression is its scalability. You can use one high-resolution master file to create lower-resolution files. Also, for editing, it uses only intraframe coding, so each video picture is built separately. As a result, it's technically far easier to edit than MPEG-based systems (including HDV), which use interframe coding that relies on predictive frames. The main disadvantage of JPEG 2000 is that it requires far more computational power than MPEG-based compression solutions.

If you don't want to use JPEG 2000, the Infinity camcorder offers optional MPEG-2 recording, which allows for SD and HD acquisition. The 25 Mbps bit stream conforms to the HDV standard, but it is not called HDV by Grass Valley. Also, its MPEG-2 files are written in an MXF-based wrapper so they can be recognized by a variety of devices and software programs.

Ikegami EditcamHD

Ikegami is a pioneer in tapeless acquisition. In 1994, the company joined forces with Avid Technology to create Editcam®. It was truly a product ahead of its time, with an expensive and cumbersome removable hard disk drive called a FieldPak®. However, technology has improved over the years, and Editcam is in its third generation. Today, the FieldPak2 weighs less than a pound and is small enough to fit in a shirt pocket. And Ikegami has established an EditcamHD family of field production camcorders.

Figure 7.4 Ikegami's EditcamHD can record using a hard disk drive (FieldPak2) or solid-state memory (RamPak). (Photo courtesy of Ikegami)

The HDN-X10 camcorder, shown in **Figure 7.4**, uses three, 2/3-inch CMOS image sensors and supports 1080i/50, 1080i/60, 1080p/24, 720p/50, and 720p/60 acquisition. A 120 GB FieldPak2 can record up to 90 minutes of 1080i/60 footage. Solid-state RamPaks® media will become available as solid-state capacities increase (and prices decrease). Ikegami's collaboration with Avid continues; the HDN-X10 uses Avid's DNxHD 145 codec to deliver 1920 × 1080 HD images on an NLE in real time. The system currently supports 8-bit sampling, but is expected to support 10-bit sampling (DNxHD 220) in the future.

Sony XDCAM HD

The HDV format is actually a part of the Sony XDCAM HD series of products, which is an expansion of the XDCAM tapeless acquisition format introduced by Sony in 2003. Both XDCAM and XDCAM HD record on Professional Disc®, a proprietary optical disc technology. XDCAM HD has been included in this chapter because it offers additional HD recording modes.

As you know, the HDV format specifications call for a 25 Mbps bit rate for recording 1080i. That bit rate does not change; it is called a constant bit rate. XDCAM HD offers two additional HD settings, 35 Mbps and 18 Mbps. These settings use variable bit rate technology, a more efficient system that reduces the bit rate when visual images are not as complex.

Sony's PFD-23 Professional Disc media capacity is 23.3 GB, almost five times the capacity of a DVD. It is enough to store more than an hour of footage at 35 Mbps, 90 minutes of HDV footage, and more than two hours of 18 Mbps. Professional Disc media is about the same size as a DVD, but it is contained in a protective cartridge. Also, unlike the red-laser technology of CDs and DVDs, the XDCAM system uses blue-laser technology, which provides much faster data transfer rates. Sony officials estimate a disc can be reused for at least 1,000 and up to 10,000 erase/write cycles, and has an archival life of more than 50 years.

Figure 7.5 Sony's initial XDCAM HD camcorders can record HD footage at a variety of bit rates. (Photo courtesy of Sony)

In a 2006 interview for *Government Video* magazine, Hugo Gaggioni, Sony's chief technology officer, Broadcast and Production Systems Division, said the two initial XDCAM HD camcorders, the PDW-F330 and the PDW-F350, represent a balance between picture quality and data rates. Both cameras feature three 1/2-inch CCDs with 12-bit processing, and both record in 1080i (with a 24p mode as well). The F350 adds variable frame rate recording (overcranking and undercranking). Sony branded XDCAM HD as part of its CineAlta product line, the same product line as its high-end HDCAM offerings. The justification is that many of the F350's features will appeal to independent filmmakers that do not have the budget for HDCAM equipment. (See **Figure 7.5**.)

However, XDCAM HD should also appeal to news environments. The camera's transport is so rugged that the operator can run while shaking the camera and the laser will not mistrack. The XDCAM product line, for example, was adopted by a number of broadcast stations before XDCAM HD was announced. Sony positioned its SD optical disc solution as an upgrade path for Betacam SP facilities and a seamless addition to DVCAM-based operations. Now, there is a clear upgrade path for these stations to move up to XDCAM HD. In fact, in early 2006 CBS announced that its owned and operated stations would make the transition to XDCAM HD for news over the next two years, starting with its Chicago-based and additional stations.

Points of Interest

- Solid-state recording may be cost prohibitive now due to the high price of recording media, but it has the potential to become the preferred industry standard.

- Sony's XDCAM HD offers HDV acquisition on optical disc, as well as other HD recording options.

- The Grass Valley Infinity Digital Media Camcorder has an MPEG-2 option for HDV-like acquisition, but is primarily focused on JPEG 2000-based HD imagery.

Workflow Considerations

None of these solutions are expected to match the picture quality of a high-end Sony HDCAM camcorder. Then again, neither does any HDV camcorder currently on the market. After all, if you could attain the identical image from an inexpensive camcorder as you could from the top-of-the line model, why would you buy something that costs 20 times as much? As the HD universe continues to expand, it becomes more obvious that all HD is not created equal. Compression, optics, and image processing, among other factors, contribute to the quality of the image. With most things, you get what you pay for—and HD camcorders are no exception.

It's no accident that these HDV alternatives are tapeless solutions. While the slow and steady move toward HD is already in progress for much of the professional video industry, there is also a migration by some facilities toward a tapeless workflow as NLEs and servers increase the prevalence of IT-based infrastructures. Footage that starts as data provides flexibility that is simply not possible with tape-based acquisition. For example, Panasonic's P2 camcorders allow you to preview clips in the field, similar to reviewing stills in a digital camera. You can sort your shots, even delete the ones you do not want, before you even sit down at your NLE. Plus, you do not have to ingest footage in real time; files can be transferred much quicker to your hard drive.

NY1, a 24-hour news cable channel operated by Time Warner in New York City, has been using Panasonic P2 camcorders since the 2004 Republican National Convention. In 2005, Joe Truncale, NY1's news director of operations and engineering, wrote that the station was impressed by the format's high-speed file transfers, elimination of ingesting (or digitizing) footage, and in-camera clip management, all of which contribute to getting video on the channel quicker and more efficiently. Although the station does not yet offer HD programming, it invested in 16 HVX200 camcorders in 2006. The camcorders will help begin an HD transition for NY1, which will likely take a couple of years.

Tapeless acquisition also requires an adjustment in thinking about budgets. For example, P2 is a recycled media, not a consumed media. You do not fill your P2 card with raw footage and retire it after a few passes. You transfer that footage into a storage device, then reuse that P2 card on your next assignment, and the next, and the next . . . for years. The initial investment is high—a few thousand dollars at least to equip each camcorder with sufficient P2 cards—but the cost savings on videotape over time can be substantial. In fact, many organizations have made the case that the P2 media should be considered part of the camera/capital budget, as opposed to the annual operating budget.

The same argument could hold for Ikegami FieldPak2 or RamPak removable drives, as well as the various FireStore hard disk drives from FOCUS Enhancements. Infinity and XDCAM systems utilize digital media designed for hundreds of rewrite cycles without the image degradation that occurs after a few passes on videotape. However, the comparative lower costs of a Professional Disc or REV PRO disk could entice facilities to use these alternatives more like traditional tape media.

Of course, you can still make a case for tape. As we discussed in Chapter 2, even high-quality HDV tape is relatively inexpensive. The transition to a tapeless facility requires a serious investment in digital storage; after all, you have to transfer all that raw footage somewhere if you plan to reuse your media. Archiving also requires consideration—what is your plan for long-term storage and access? And you'll probably need to invest in some sort of digital asset management system so you can find the various digital files in your system.

Storage considerations aside, the HDV alternatives from Panasonic, Grass Valley, Ikegami, and Sony provide further options to HD content producers on a budget. While these options might be more expensive than some of the tape-based HDV camcorders on the market, they are also significantly less expensive than high-end HD cameras, such as Sony HDCAM models and Panasonic's Varicam. The larger, shoulder-mounted models are designed specifically to appeal to ENG operations. In addition, these alternatives embrace a tapeless workflow that can improve efficiency and potentially reduce media costs in the long run.

Points of Interest

- All HD is not created equal; image quality varies considerably based on optics, compression, and image processing.

- Some tapeless recording media are very expensive but could be more cost efficient than videotape as a long-term solution.

- Tapeless technologies can improve workflow efficiency through faster file transfer times and immediate access to footage.

Conclusion

Working with HDV is more than just buying a new camcorder. For video professionals, there are new workflow options, artistic issues, production considerations, and editing and delivery concerns. Whether you choose HDV or another low-cost HD format, you still need to figure out the best way to capitalize on that investment. We hope this book has been a helpful part of the process. The HDV format gives you a conduit to produce outstanding HD imagery at a reasonable price point. How you maximize its potential is up to you.

GLOSSARY

3:2 pulldown. A process that takes four film frames and creates ten video fields for interlaced playback.

24p. 24 frames progressive. A popular frame rate for video acquisition that attempts to imitate the motion of film.

Artifacts. Unwanted elements or defects in a video picture.

Aspect Ratio. The ratio of the width of the screen to the height of the screen. HDV has a 16:9 aspect ratio, while most standard definition formats have a 4:3 aspect ratio. See also *Widescreen*.

ATSC. Advanced Television Systems Committee. A nonprofit organization established to develop voluntary standards for DTV. The FCC adopted a modified version of its DTV standard for U.S. broadcasters in 1996.

Backlighting. When the strongest light source comes from behind the subject and the foreground object becomes silhouette.

Bandwidth. The information-carrying capacity of a television channel or video signal. The ATSC DTV pipeline, for example, carries about 19.39 Mbps of data.

Bit. Binary digit. The smallest unit of data in a binary system, either a zero or a one. See also *byte*.

Bit Rate. The amount of data that moves through a digital system. Expressed as bits per second or bps. Reduced through compression.

Blu-ray DVD. A new type of HD DVD which holds approximately 25 gigabytes of data per side.

Byte. A group of bits that is processed together. The more bits in a byte, the more distinct the values in that byte. See also *Bit*.

CCD. Charge Coupled Device. One type of chip within a camera that collects light and converts it into electrical impulses. See also *CMOS*.

CMOS. Complementary Metal Oxide Semiconductor. A newer, more light sensitive chip technology for cameras that produces less heat and uses less power than CCDs. See also *CCD*.

Chrominance. The color information in a shot.

CineFrame 24. Sony's variant of 24p that shoots at 60i and imitates 24p.

CineFrame 25. Sony's variant of 25p that shoots at 50i and imitates 25p (mainly for the UK).

CineFrame 30. Sony's "film look" that imitates progressive scan while shooting interlaced footage.

CinemaScope. A widescreen theatrical display format (2:35 to 1) developed in 1953 to lure patrons away from television and back into the movie theatres.

Component. A cable for video only where the signal is split into three different signals.

Composite. A cable for video where color and luminance information are sent together.

Compression. Used in digital video to reduce the size of video files by removing redundant or noncritical data. See also *Interframe* and *Intraframe*.

DTV. Digital Television. A new television broadcast transmission standard that provides better images than NTSC as well as the potential for additional services. See also *Datacasting* and *Multicasting*.

DVD-5. A DVD containing 4.7 gigabytes of information on one side of the disc.

DVD-9. Either a dual layer disc or double-sided DVD containing almost nine gigabytes of information.

Datacasting. Transmission of data, such as graphics and text, in the DTV stream for non-broadcast use. See also *DTV*.

Defragment. Clearing your hard drive of random files that may be disbursed throughout the drive.

Downconversion. Converting footage with higher resolution into a format with less resolution, such as HD to SD. See also *Upconversion* and *Transcode*.

Duplication. When a DVD is copied or cloned using a recordable DVD. This type of DVD is not compatible in all DVD players.

Edge Crop. An HD 16:9 image that has been downconverted to SD with the left and right edges of the image cropped to fill a 4:3 frame. See also *Letterbox*, *Pan and Scan*, and *Squeeze*.

ED. Enhanced Definition. Provides better resolution (480p) than SD monitors, but does not provide enough lines of resolution to be considered high definition.

FCC. Federal Communications Commission. An agency of the U.S. government established by the Communications Act of 1934 that regulates television, satellite, and cable communications.

FireWire. A four or six-pin cable that is used to transfer video and audio to and from a camcorder, VTR, or a storage medium. Also known as IEEE-1394 or iLink.

Frame. One complete image, used in a series of images to create the illusion of motion.

Frame Rate. The number of frames of video shown per second. See also *Frame*.

GOP. Group of Pictures. Interrelated images used in MPEG-2 compression that rely on motion estimation between frames to reduce file sizes. Can contain intracoded (I), predictive (P), and bi-directional predictive (B) frames. See also *Compression*.

HD. High Definition. Video with significantly more lines of resolution than SD. There are two distinct systems, 1080i (1,080 interlaced lines of resolution) and 720p (720 progressive lines of resolution). See also *ED* and *SD*.

HD-DVD. A new format of DVD capable of holding 15 gigabytes of information per side (created for HD use).

HDV. A high definition video format established in 2003 that has been adopted for low-cost HD acquisition.

Hypergain. Sony's way of boosting the low light level gain above –18dB.

iLink. Sony's name for FireWire (IEEE-1394) connectivity. See also *FireWire*.

Image Stabilization. Circuitry in modern camcorders that helps eliminate some of the unsteadiness in handheld shots.

Interframe. Compression that groups sequences of video frames together to remove redundant information. See also *Compression* and *Intraframe*.

Intraframe. Compression that is self-contained within an individual frame and encodes only the differences between pixels. Used in DV compression and in I frames in MPEG-2 compression. See also *Compression* and *Interframe*.

Interlaced Scanning. A form of video compression that forms frames from two interlaced fields of alternating lines. Used in the NTSC transmission standard and some video formats. See also *Progressive Scanning*.

Letterbox. 16:9 aspect ratio footage displayed on a 4:3 monitor with black bands at the top and bottom of the screen. See also *Edge Crop, Pan and Scan*, and *Squeeze*.

Lossless. Compression that removes redundant information to reduce file sizes, but restores all original data to create an exact duplicate of the original. See also *Lossy*.

Lossy. Bit rate reduction accomplished by discarding unnecessary data. In digital video, provides higher compression ratios than lossless compression schemes, but creates an approximation, not an exact duplicate, of the original image. See also *Lossless*.

Luminance. The portion of the video signal that determines the light and dark areas of the video image.

MPEG-2. Compression system developed by the Motion Picture Experts Group that uses a combination of intraframe and interframe technologies.

Multicasting. Transmitting two or more program streams simultaneously in a DTV signal. See also *DTV*.

NTSC. National Television Standards Committee. The television format used in the United States and Japan. The system includes 525 lines of horizontal resolution, 30 interlaced frames per second, and 60 Hz. The aspect ratio is 4:3.

Oversampling. The practice of shooting in HD and downconverting footage to SD, thus improving the quality of the SD image (overshooting originally in SD). More generally, when an image is acquired and manipulated at a resolution higher than it will be distributed to optimize image quality. See also *Downconversion*.

PAL. Phase Alteration of Line. The broadcast transmission format used in Europe. The system includes 625 lines of horizontal resolution, 25 interlaced frames per second, and 50 Hz. The aspect ratio is 4:3.

Pan and Scan. Using an HD 16:9 image that has been downconverted to SD, a computer determines what action in the frame should be displayed on a 4:3 screen and pans to that part of the image accordingly. See also *Edge Crop*, *Letterbox*, and *Squeeze*.

Persistence of Vision. The physiological occurrence that allows a series of still images shown in rapid succession to appear to be in motion. See also *Frame Rate*.

Progressive Scanning. A process where all lines of a frame of video are transmitted consecutively. Used for computer displays and some video formats. See also *Interlaced Scanning*.

Quantization. The number of bits used in a digital sample of an analog signal.

RCA Connections. The video signal is usually carried over the yellow-colored connection and a stereo audio signal is carried over the red and white connections. This signal is slightly better than RF cable because the video and audio signals are split.

RF Cable. Radio frequency coaxial cable which connects a deck to a monitor. The video and audio signal are carried in the same cable. This is the lowest-quality connection.

RAID. Redundant Array of Independent Discs. A type of storage drive (or group of drives) which quickly stores information in various places on the drives.

Replication. A DVD that is copied or created from a glass master in a dust-free environment. This type of disc is playable in all DVD players.

S-Video. A cable that splits the chrominance and luminance in the same cable for a sharper image. Audio is not carried through this cable.

Safe Area. The area in a video frame in which the main action should occur. Going beyond these boundaries may mean some monitors will not display what has been shot. Often used a guideline for 16:9 footage that is expected to be displayed in 4:3.

Sampling. The process of measuring an analog signal so it can be converted into a digital signal. See also *Sampling Frequency*.

Sampling Frequency. The number of discrete digital samples of an analog signal per second during an analog-to-digital conversion. See also *Sampling*.

SD. Standard Definition. The resolution of the NTSC broadcast standard, 480 interlaced lines of resolution.

Selective Colorization. Highlighting one particular color (such as red) in a black-and-white scene.

Squeeze. 16:9 aspect ratio footage displayed in 4:3 with the image squeezed to fit into that frame size. See also *Edge Crop, Letterbox,* and *Pan and Scan*.

Tapeless Acquisition. Recording images and sound on something other than videotape, such as a hard disk drive, solid-state memory, or optical disc.

Transcode. Conversion of a video signal from one format to another. See also *Downconversion* and *Upconversion*.

Upconversion. Converting footage with lower image resolution to a format with higher resolution, such as SD to HD. See also *Downconversion* and *Transcode*.

VHS. Vertical Helical Scan or Video Home System. A cassette-based consumer video standard.

Widescreen. Footage that fills a 16:9 screen. See also *Aspect Ratio*.

Bibliography

"A day in the life of HDV." *Showreel* (online), www.showreel.org, Winter 2005.

"A Public Policy History of HDTV." National Cable & Telecommunications Association, June 2003.

Ankeney, Jay. "HDV Everywhere." *Computer Graphics World*, November 2005, pp. 8–10.

Barber, Kirk. *The Wedding Video Handbook*. San Francisco: CMP Books, 2005.

Book, Constance Ledoux. *Digital Television: DTV and the Consumer*. Ames, Iowa: Blackwell Publishing, 2004.

Braverman, Barry. *Video Shooter: Storytelling with DV, HD and HDV Cameras*. San Francisco: CMP Books, 2005.

Brice, Richard. *Newnes Guide to Digital TV, 2nd Edition*. Oxford, England: Newnes, 2003.

Careless, James. "The Death of Proprietary Recording Media?" *Television Broadcast*, September 2005, pp. 10–13.

Davis, Bill. "Timeline: HDV Editing!" *Videomaker*, March 2005, p. 56.

DVD Players: CE Market Overview Report. Consumer Electronics Association, December 2005.

Eagle, Douglas Spotted. *HDV: What You NEED to Know, 2nd Edition.* Stockton, UT: VASST/Sundance Media Group, Inc., 2006.

Giardina, Carolyn. "Addressing FAQ's – Including Several HD Misconceptions." *SHOOT*, Feburary 10, 2006, pp. 16–17.

Gibby, Steve. "Panasonic AG-HVX200: The Choice for Any Style Production." *Studio/monthly*, April 2006, pp. 26–28.

Gloman, Chuck. "The Little Things." *Government Video,* December 2005.

Gloman, Chuck. "JVC Offers More than a Handful." *Government Video,* March 2006.

Gloman, Chuck. "Great HDV Expectations." *Videography,* April 2006, pp. 52–55.

Grotticelli, Michael. "Grass Valley's new Infinity production platform." *Broadcast Engineering,* September 1, 2005.

Grotticelli, Michael. "WAY Beyond Videotape." *Film & Video* (online), www.studiodaily.com, January 1, 2006.

HDV Technology Handbook. San Diego: Sony Corporation, 2004.

Kerschbaumer, Ken. "Grass Valley Goes Tapeless." *Broadcasting & Cable,* September 12, 2005, p. 36.

Kerschbaumer, Ken. "HDV Camcorders Ready for Prime Time." *Broadcasting & Cable*, February 21, 2005, p. 18.

Kerschbaumer, Ken. "P2 Report Card: So Far So Good." *Broadcasting & Cable*, March 27, 2006.

Lock, Andrew. *How to Shoot, Edit & Distribute HDV*. Orange, CA: The Focal Point Publishing Company, 2006.

Martinez, Juan. "Development of high-performance HDV devices based on the HDV 1080i specification for acquisition and production applications (white paper)." Sony Electronics, 2005.

Nordhal, Tore B. "Cost Effective 1/3" CCD HD Camcorders: Analyzing mature HD formats & emerging HDV & comparing acquisition capabilities." *Nordhal HDTV Report* (online), www.coax.tv, 2006.

Nordhal, Tore B.. "Analyzing new and emerging HD Storage and Compression formats, and forecasting dominant professional implementations through 2010." *Nordhal HDTV Report* (online), www.coax.tv, 2006.

Pescatore, Mark J. "Everyone's an HD critic." *Government Video*, February 2006, p. 4.

Pescatore, Mark J. "Broadcast options for the transition to digital television." *Feedback* 40 (4), 1999, pp. 1–7.

Pescatore, Mark J. and Zappier, Alicia. "The new format war." *Government Video*, July 2003, pp. 12–15.

Rothman, Wilson. "Gadget of the Week: Sanyo HD1 Digital Media Camera." *Time* (online), www.time.com, April 5, 2006.

Silbergleid, Michael and Pescatore, Mark J. (Eds.) *The Guide to Digital Television, 3rd Edition.* New York: Miller Freeman PSN, 2000.

Soltz, Ned and Kadner, Noah. "Are We Looking at a Tapeless HD Future?" *Videography,* May 2005, pp. 20–25.

Stevenson, Cammy. "JVC JY-HD10U Mini DV Digital Camcorder." Newbie (online), *www.newbie.net*

Todorovic', Aleksandar Louis. *Television Technology Demystified.* Burlington, MA: Focal Press, 2006.

Truncale, Joe. "NY1 News goes tapeless with Panasonic's P2 recording system." *Broadcast Engineering,* March 1, 2005.

Watkinson, John. *An Introduction to Digital Video, 2nd Edition.* Oxford: Focal Press, 2001.

Weise, Marcus and Weynand, Diana. *How Video Works.* Burlington, MA: Focal Press, 2004.

Wargo, Sean. "The Changing TV Market." Presented at the Entertainment Technology Policy Summit, March 15–16, 2006.

Index